W9-AMC-334

Read These Too

Snowballs in the Bookdrop
(W.M., 1982)

Bibliotoons
(G.H., McFarland, 1990)

Unintellectual Freedoms
(W.M., McFarland, 1991)

Unprofessional Behavior
(W.M. & G.H., McFarland, 1992)

Unsolicited Advice
(W.M. & G.H., McFarland, 1992)

For Library Directors Only
(W.M. & R. Lee, McFarland, 1993)

For Library Trustees Only
(W.M. & R. Lee, McFarland, 1993)

The Manley Art of Librarianship
(W.M., McFarland, 1993)

Unsolicited Advice

Observations of a Public Librarian

By Will Manley

Illustrations By Gary Handman

McFarland & Company, Inc., Publishers
Jefferson, North Carolina and London

British Library Cataloguing-in-Publication data are available

Library of Congress Cataloguing-in-Publication Data

Manley, Will, 1949–
Unsolicited advice : observations of
a public librarian / by Will Manley;
illustrations by Gary Handman.
Includes index.
ISBN 0-89950-745-X (lib. bdg. : 50# alk. paper) ∞
1. Library administration – United States – Humor.
2. Public libraries – United States – Administration – Humor.
I. Handman, Gary, 1950–
II. Title.
Z678.M2795 1992
027.4′0973
92-50311
CIP

McFarland & Company, Inc., Publishers
Box 611, Jefferson, North Carolina 28640

Table of Contents

Don't Make the Coffee Too Hot or Too Strong

Dear Stumped,

Our lives are an unlikely combination of the sublime and the ridiculous–99 percent ridiculous and 1 percent sublime. Despite what we read on our Hallmark cards, the human condition is not best described by vague abstractions. Our lives tend to be less guided by theoretical concepts like justice, love, and honor and more by the immediate realities of a dead car battery, a malfunctioning refrigerator, or a teenage son out till three in the morning.

The questions and challenges that we face each day are not the big issues of philosophy or theology. When we wake up in the morning we do not muse on the existence of God or the nature of reality. Instead our attention is taken up with deciding what tie to wear, determining whether or not the furnace is making a funny noise again, and trying to remember to take the chicken out of the freezer for tonight's dinner.

It is usually after a series of mundane mishaps like dropping a carton of milk on the floor, slipping in the shower, and cutting ourselves shaving that we step back from the chaos of our lives and ask ourselves, "What's it all about?" Our propensity for philosophy is, therefore, borne more out of a feeling of frustration than in a sense of wonderment.

Most of us live lives of little cosmic importance. Very few of us do anything so big or so bad as to merit even passing mention on the nightly news. What satisfaction we enjoy in life is not derived from helping to establish world peace or from discovering a way to fix the hole in the ozone layer, but rather from making the right decisions about the little things, such as pulling our frozen dinner out of the microwave at precisely the right moment.

Our library work lives are no different from our private lives. Grandiose professional principles take a back seat to our 8 to 5 creature comforts. "Is the coffee too hot or too strong?" is often of more concern to us than the latest theories of participative management, and whether we are physically comfortable at our computer workstation is of greater immediate importance than the effectiveness of the latest on-line search strategy. It's not that the big issues of librarianship are meaningless, it's just that the little things – the everyday conundrums of library existence – take precedence.

That's the impression I get when I find myself in the middle of a dialog about libraries with other librarians. Concerns about national information policy and the other big professional issues of our time are almost always ignored in favor of the little things like latchkey children, Sunday hours, staff room etiquette, and men's room hand drivers. The irony of course is that rarely do the things that really matter to librarians ever get bandied about in our professional literature, and that is precisely why most professional literature largely goes unread.

This book attempts to be different. It attempts to address the 99 percent of our professional lives that is ridiculous. If the 1 percent sublime leaks forth, well, no one's perfect.

If has taken me quite a long time to appreciate the importance of the ridiculous. Over the years as a writer and speaker it has been my own self-important desire to address the big issues of librarianship. But grudgingly I came to realize that far more people were interested when I wrote about bookdrop abuse than when I wrote about intellectual freedom and far more people stayed awake when I spoke about the problems with electric pencil sharpeners than when I spoke about the problems with computerized bibliographic networks.

Several eons ago when I was a reference librarian it was an unending source of frustration for me that I never got asked highly intellectual research questions. I was offended that people wanted to know more about dogs than dogmatic theology. Today I am frustrated that when librarians write to me or talk to me they would rather ask questions about microwave ovens than microfilm periodical collections.

But I have not forgotten their questions. They are recreated in this book in a kind of random mosaic. Somewhere in this chaos of everyday conundrums there is a meaning, but I have no idea what it is.

Let me know if you figure it out.

Regards,
Will

Librarians in Drag Should Only Come Out on Halloween Night

Dear Will,

I am fortunate to have the most progressive, most enthusiastic, and most humanistic reference staff in the entire world. These six professionals (three men, three women) are fabulous. At Christmas time they adopted a needy family, and on Earth Day they set up a recycling center in the library parking lot. They have also developed a most creative series of "how to use the library" programs based on a Saturday Night Live comedy format.

Their latest idea, however, gives me pause to say the least. Remember the time Phil Donahue dressed up in drag for his show on transvestites? That's basically what my reference librarians want to do for National Library Week. The three men want to dress up as women, and the three women want to masquerade as men.

The rationale behind all of this is "consciousness raising." The men want to experience firsthand how women are treated at the reference desk and the women want to get a feel for how people regard male librarians.

I will admit that their intentions are quite noble, but really I am repulsed by the utter kinkiness of it all. That's my purely visceral feeling about the whole thing.

But there are larger issues beyond my own personal feelings — such as political considerations. What if word leaks out, as it inevitably will, to the City Council that there is some serious cross-dressing going on down at the public library with full administrative backing. What happens when the story gets on the front page of the newspaper?

On the other hand, I pride myself for being an open administrator committed to participative management. I have always encouraged my library staff to think creatively and act independently. The last thing I want to do is stifle initiative and hurt morale.

Any ideas?

Sincerely,
WORRIED

Dear Worried,

If your library is located in California, I'd say go ahead and let your reference librarians do their thing. In any of the other 49 states I'd restrict such an experiment to Halloween night.

Best regards,
Will

*   *   *

Eating Yogurt with a Straw Is Not a Socially Acceptable Practice

Dear Will,

I am a reference librarian in a small academic library and ordinarily I wouldn't worry about such a thing but the eating habits of one of my co-workers (a cataloger) makes it impossible for me to make use of the staff lounge during my regularly scheduled lunch break. Because we have such a small staff that is spread so thin, it is impossible to change my break to another time. I either have to endure this man or eat my lunch in the bathroom.

Don't get me wrong. This cataloger seems to be a very nice man and I am told that his cataloging work is of the highest quality, but, Will, quite frankly it makes me sick to my stomach when he sucks his yogurt through a straw. Not only is it thoroughly disgusting to

think about someone sucking yogurt through a straw, it is even more loathsome to actually watch and listen to it happen.

The first time I witnessed this spectacle I grimaced and asked the cataloger to use a spoon. He ignored me like he didn't understand English and continued to suck happily away. I hoped that this was an aberration. It wasn't. Everyday for the next three weeks he sucked yogurt through a straw for lunch. That's when I began eating my lunch in the bathroom.

Fortunately or unfortunately, I am the only one affected by this problem. Everyone else on the library staff has a different lunch schedule. To make the problem worse, this man is from Southeast Asia. He emigrated to this country during the Vietnam War. Because I am respectful of other cultures, I do not want to offend him by pressing this issue. For all I know sucking yogurt through a straw may be a socially acceptable practice in his homeland.

What should I do?

Sincerely,

THERE OUGHTA BE A LAW

Dear Oughta,

I have done an on-line search of legal reference materials and have determined that sucking yogurt through a straw is a perfectly legal thing to do and will probably continue to be so well into the foreseeable future.

Just because something is legal, however, does not make it tolerable, and I would hate to think of what Emily Post or Judith Martin would say about this peculiar practice.

Your concern that this cataloger is simply following the customs of his native land is unfounded. After doing an extensive reference search I could find nothing that would indicate that Southeast Asians typically suck yogurt through a straw. The issue should not, therefore, be complicated by cultural sensibilities.

In a nutshell, although it's somewhat off-beat, I consider this issue to be a very important one. Your staff lounge should function as a kind of sanctum sanctorum, a place where overworked and underpaid library staffers can relax and unwind. The atmosphere of the lounge should work to alleviate job stress, not exacerbate it. You should not have to endure the nausea that results from watching a cataloger suck yogurt through a straw.

My advice, therefore, is to confront the problem head-on. Sit down with this man and tell him that his eating habits are highly offensive. Explain to him that from your own experience you know that yogurt can be greatly enjoyed with a spoon. In fact to show your good will, you might even present him with a gift wrapped box of plastic spoons (preferably a year's supply if you can afford it).

If you do not feel comfortable with the directness of this approach then you should see your library director. Ask him or her to put out to *all* staff members a memo putting forth the rules and regulations governing the use of the staff lounge. By putting the memo out to everyone, the yogurt sucker will not feel picked on. The memo should read like this:

STAFF ROOM RULES
1. Always clean up the microwave.
2. Always refill the coffee pot when it is empty.
3. Always throw away uneaten food.
4. Never suck yogurt through a straw.

If your cataloger still doesn't get the message, you have my permission to assassinate him.

Regards,
Will

Better a Basketball Hoop on the Office Wall Than a Bottle of Bourbon in the Desk Drawer

Dear Will,

I am the president of the board of trustees for a large East Coast public library. From all indications our rather young director (he's

35) is doing a good job of handling the many responsibilities that are involved in managing a large, urban public library. He's a personable young man. The board likes him, the city council likes him, and the staff likes him. Furthermore, our library usage indicators (circulation, registration, etc.) have all increased significantly since he came on board.

But I still have one serious reservation about him. He has mounted a Nerf basketball hoop on his office wall. This, I think, detracts from his professionalism. I have always felt that an executive's office should be neat, dignified, and businesslike. All office accoutrements should give off a sense of seriousness of purpose. The basketball hoop does just the opposite. It gives his office the ambience of a college dorm room.

But that is not all that bothers me. He actually plays with the hoop! Over the past two months I have wandered unannounced into his office ten or eleven times. On seven of those occasions I caught him shooting a small, spongy ball at the hoop. He even has the net wired so that when he makes a basket, he is rewarded with a cheering noise.

My concerns are twofold: (1) he is not giving off the proper image and (2) he is obviously frittering away his time unproductively. If he were not doing such a good job I would not hesitate to demand that he take the hoop down. But it does, by all accounts, seem as though he is performing well. What should I do?

Sincerely,
CONCERNED BUT NOT PANICKED

Dear Concerned,

This is an easy one. Directing a large urban public library is a very difficult, very stressful job. You're lucky to have found such a good person to fill the job. You don't want to lose him by bugging him with fussbudget criticism.

One of the reasons he is such a good director is that he obviously knows how to manage stress constructively. That's what the basket-ball hoop is for—letting off steam. It's much healthier than hiding a bottle of bourbon in the desk drawer.

Leave the man alone!

Regards,
Will

If Your Janitor Is Scared of a Glow in the Dark Jesus, He's Got a Guilty Conscience

Dear Will,

One of our catalogers is a religious fanatic. She has converted her work area into a kind of mini shrine complete with crosses, Bibles, and a glow in the dark picture of Jesus. This makes many of our staff uncomfortable.

Furthermore, she never misses an opportunity to talk religion at social events, in the staff lounge, and even during staff meetings. Lately she has been putting out a monthly newsletter, entitled *The Divine Interface*. To give you a flavor of this publication, the first issue started out by declaring that "God is the ultimate cataloger. At the endtime he will classify us all as either sheep or goats." She passes this newsletter out to everyone on staff and even sends it out to other libraries.

When we have meetings of our collection development task force (of which she is a member) she constantly raises questions about why we don't acquire more books from Christian publishing houses. This always starts an emotional argument and puts everyone into a bad mood.

In this woman's defense, I will say that she has never spent library money or library time on her newsletter, and she has never been openly insubordinate. For instance, she has never refused to catalog a book because it was sacrilegious, blasphemous, or anti-Christian.

But frankly, Will, this woman has been getting on my nerves and everyone else's. Do you think it is time for me to sit down and suggest she start cooling the God bit? She is a nice and gentle soul but sometimes that type of person can really drive you crazy.

And, oh yes, our janitor, who comes in to clean the library after hours, is spooked by the glow in the dark Jesus. He claims that wherever he goes the eyes in the picture follow him. Should I make her take the picture down?

Sincerely,

TRYING TO KEEP AN OPEN MIND

Dear Open,

First about the janitor. It sounds like he's got a guilty conscience about something. If he really thinks that this glow in the dark Jesus is keeping an eagle eye on him, that's all to your advantage. Think of how much cleaner your building will be. Myself, I'd work a lot harder

if I had Jesus staring at me all the time. Maybe every library should
have one.

As for your cataloger, what's the big deal? Her only sin in your
eyes is that she is very religious. Since when is being religious a sin?
Consider yourself lucky. The woman is not a drunk, a druggie, or a
sex maniac.

Your letter points up an unfortunate truth about librarians. Our
profession is not real comfortable with religion in general. Many
librarians identify religion with censorship because Jerry Falwell and
his followers are so notorious for keeping a close eye on what we do
and what we don't acquire for our book collections. The religious
right and the intellectual freedom extremists have gone to battle
many times.

But all of this should not be held against your holy cataloger.
From your letter I have to conclude that she is more interested in
promoting Christian books than in banning non–Christian ones.
What's the problem in that? There is not a librarian in the world who
is not biased in the area of book collection development. Librarians
who are interested in needlepoint tend to order an inordinate
number of books on needlepoint and those passionate about skiing
tend to order lots of skiing books. This woman's interest just happens to be in the area of religion.

And as far as her proselytizing goes, how's that different from
anything else? I have a friend who is nuts about the opera, and he is
always going around raving about this performance or that performance. In fact he spends a lot of his time trying to persuade the rest
of us to go with him. Personally, I'd rather watch home shopping
spree on cable, but I don't reprimand the guy for being enthusiastic
about something no one else cares about. And with regard to the
newsletter, you wouldn't want to interfere with her intellectual
freedom, would you? The First Amendment works for everyone. My
advice, therefore, is to be fair. Don't judge this woman with a double
standard.

Finally, you have to ask yourself what's the world coming to
when bosses feel the need to chastise their employees for being too
religious.

Shalom,

Will

If Your Reference Librarian Shows Up to Work in a Giorgio Armani Suit, You May Have Problems

Dear Will,

All librarians should read! If I were to make one criticism about the new librarians coming out of library school it is that they do not read! They tinker and they hack and they play with their computers, but they do not read!

Well, I can tell you that they won't work for me! I no longer hire people with M.L.S. degrees! I want people who are avid readers – the kind of people who read during breakfast, lunch, dinner, and sex. Why – because I believe that the reader's advisory function is still the most important service we provide, and so my reference librarians darn well better know the best book to consult for pouring a concrete slab and they sure as heck better know which cookbook has the best recipe for fried bananas. Librarianship is not a job or a profession. It is a passion for books.

Our reference librarians, therefore, do not simply point the patrons in the direction of the book stacks. As knowledgeable professionals they are trained to make definite recommendations. I expect them to know that when it comes to home repairs that Elbert Hubbel is still tops and that you can't beat Martha Stewart when it comes to entertaining and decorating. Acquiring this knowledge takes time, dedication, and passion. Anything less is simply unacceptable.

This is basically the message that I give to each new reference librarian on his or her first day. From the very beginning I want to kindle a passion for reading. With Fred, however, I kindled more than a passion. He's become a raging bonfire that is quickly getting out of control.

Fred came on board seven months ago. His problem is that he not only reads books, he lives them. For instance, he read a book on power dressing and went out and bought a Giorgio Armani suit and tried to charge it to the library. Then he read a Bob Villa book and bought a bunch of tools and made an offer on an old rundown house. Fortunately the deal fell through – his credit was bad because of the $2,000 he spent on the Armani suit. Then he started reading Hemingway and shortly thereafter he started drinking and fighting and womanizing.

Now we're scared. Now our literary chameleon is reading *American Psycho* by Brett Easton Ellis. This is the controversial book about a serial killer who daubs Grey Poupon on the brains of his victims and then sits down to dinner.

Any advice?

Sincerely,
PASSIONATE ABOUT BOOKS

Dear Passionate,

Keep the Grey Poupon in the staff lounge locked up.

Regards,
Will

Better a Moose's Head on the Boardroom Wall Than Your Own

Dear Will,

I am the director of a medium-sized Midwestern public library, and I'll be honest with you, our library does not have the biggest budget or the best book collection in the world. However, we do take great pride in our boardroom.

Some years ago, one of our long time board members died of a

sudden heart attack. When his will was read we were all pleasantly surprised to learn that he had decided to leave $50,000 to the library. This sense of joy turned to ambivalence, however, when we learned that the $50,000 was earmarked for one specific purpose— the remodeling of the boardroom.

Although there were ninety-nine other things that I would have rather spent the money on, the wishes of the deceased were closely followed under the watchful eye of the attorney handling the estate. Per the written instructions of the will, solid cherry wainscotting was installed, a fancy marble board table was built exactly according to specifications, and expensive Italian leather chairs were ordered. The results were stunning—a boardroom that could rival that of IBM or General Motors.

You really do feel special sitting in that room, and our trustees really love it. Unfortunately, the deceased overlooked one important detail in his instructions—wall decorations. Although $5,000 were specified for this purpose, no instructions were given as to the kind of wall hangings to be purchased.

Tragically, our board president got it into his mind that we should hang animal heads from the wall. It was his sudden desire to have the head of a deer, a bear, a ram, and, God forbid, even a moose mounted above the beautiful cherry wainscotting. He felt that this would give the room an exclusive club–like atmosphere.

Unfortunately the rest of the board went along with him. The vote was five to four in favor of the heads. All the men on the board voted in the affirmative, and all the women voted in the negative. I know for a fact that one of the men was opposed to the idea but he voted for it because he didn't want to look like a wimp.

Since I am absolutely certain that these animal heads will make our beautiful boardroom appear to be cheap and vulgar, I am very reluctant to implement the board's directive. To me it's like putting on a pair of rattlesnake cowboy boots when you're wearing a Brooks Brothers suit.

What should I do?

Sincerely,
APPALLED BY VULGARITY

Dear Appalled,

There is nothing that you can do. If the library board has the right to decorate the boardroom (which it does), then it has the right to use poor taste in doing so. It is the trustees' job to make policy, and it is your job to execute this policy. If you do not execute this policy, you will be the one executed and the board will have one more head to put on its wall.

By the way, all hell will break loose from the animal rights people the minute those heads are mounted. Do not allow yourself to be pulled into the ensuing controversy. Let the board president handle it. It was, after all, his policy. His head should be on the line, not yours.

Good Luck,
Will

*   *   *

Mathematics Is More Useful in Determining the Possibility That an On-line Searcher Is a Serial Wife Killer Than in Proving the Existence of God

Dear Will,

Quick question. I think I'm in love. No, I know I'm in love. It shows you the power of fate and the sometimes prescient wisdom of your supervisor. Four months ago she required me to go to a morning seminar on Boolean search- ing. I hate the whole concept of Boolean searching— the overlapping circles, the ever constricting nexus, and the utterly ruthless litany of key words—it takes all of the romance out of reference work. Whatever happened to spontaneity, intuition, and serendipity. Reference used to be an art, and I its Mary Cassatt. Now it's like turning on the micro- wave or taking your infirm aunt's tempera- ture with one of those digital thermometers that you can buy at Drug Emporium for 19¢. Where is the sense of adventure, that wonderful feeling of embarking on uncharted seas? Now it's all so clinical that you're tempted to wear a white lab coat to work.

Fortunately at this Boolean seminar I was paired off with a man who actually had a sense of compassion for my feeling of contempt for the computer and my obvious shame at not being able to master it. He was an on-line searcher employed by a university library located in a neighboring city. Handsome, competent, and polite, this man named Jack took instant pity on me when he realized how dreadfully computer illiterate I really am. With his help I muddled passably through the workshop and was grudgingly granted my cer- tificate of completion, which surprised my supervisor no end.

In appreciation for his help I offered to buy my companion lunch. To my surprise he accepted, and that afternoon we ended up eating escargot at a cozy little place near the University called Interstices.

My feelings of gratitude toward him evolved into a vague sense of personal interest when he admitted to a certain fondness for reading the Old Testament prophets. Up until then I had seen Jack as just another alien from computerland who had invaded my once bookish profession. But his predilection for scripture had the effect of rounding off some of his straight and sharpened edges. A computer whiz in love with God. This interested me. Usually they are so utterly soulless.

"Actually," Jack began, "it all started when I was a freshman at Notre Dame. They have this archaic requirement there that you must take two courses in theology regardless of your major. The first course I took was the one that all computer science students took. It was called 'Mathematical Proofs for the Existence of God.' In it you develop a series of computer models to investigate the possibility that there might be an underlying mathematical precision to the universe that would imply the existence of an omniscient creator. The emphasis was definitely on God being the Ultimate Nerd with the proverbial slide rule swinging from his belt. What you run up against with this type of approach, however, is overload. There simply isn't a computer big enough to crunch all the numbers that need to be crunched in order to establish a data base sufficiently large to plausibly establish an image of God as the Master Mathematician. It's the old Tower of Babel syndrome. God simply won't let himself be corralled by man in a logical, rational, controlled fashion."

"Actually I'm a realist," he continued. "Computers and quantitative data do have their limits. Take Pascal – now there's a man who qualifies for the Mathematics Hall of Fame – he rejected the entire numerical approach to God. He was strictly a sackcloth and ashes type of guy. In fact a lot of fairly respectable philosophers think that the whole existential movement started with Pascal's radically visceral approach to God."

"Pascal was my undergraduate hero. His writings are what ultimately landed me in Father McKenzie's Old Testament prophets class. It was during Vietnam and besides being such wonderful curmudgeons, the prophets were so uncannily relevant with their self righteous inveighing against the corruption and wickedness of those on the exalted thrones of worldly power."

Jack talked like that for hours. His biblical commentaries were particularly impressive when interspersed with all his chatter about roms, rams, megabytes, authority files, keyword indexing, and bibliographic control. I quickly began to realize how rare Jack was. He was definitely the prototypical man of the nineties, a kind of Renaissance man for the age of the computer. It was almost like God was his next-door neighbor because he would say things like Woody Allen was God's favorite filmmaker and that God really got a kick out of Andrew Dice Clay.

As time went on I began to realize that Jack's Godtalk was not his only endearing quality. Among other things he appeared to be a passable racquetball player and a competent French chef. But it really was his closeness to God that made me fall so profoundly in love with him. There is, after all, something wonderfully reassuring about being in love with a man who can teach you the intricacies of on-line searching without making it sound like a gall bladder operation and yet whose best buddy is G-O-D.

It came as a shock, therefore, three months after our initial lunch at Interstices to learn that Jack had been married twice before. Certainly lots of men his age (42) have two ex-wives but Jack was so polite, so considerate, so gentle, so moral (absolutely no sex outside of marriage), so blasted Godly that I simply couldn't conceive of him not having a successful marriage. Not that I wasn't overjoyed that he was single and available for moi.

Several nights later I got the rest of the unsettling story of Jack's two marriages. "It was God's will," he said forthrightly. "My wives both died." Then he launched into this painful yarn about how his life resonated with this incredible Job-like angst. The diatribe ended with his invitation to me to be wife numero tres. "Third time's the charm," he said with a nervous laugh when he saw that I wasn't exactly jumping up for joy.

Naturally I was more than just a little taken aback when he went on to explain that both of his wives had drowned—one while they were deep-sea fishing off the Keys and one while they were swimming across a narrow lake in the south of France. "You're not spooked, are you?" he asked when he saw the alarmed look on my face.

"No," I lied, "I'm not spooked, I'm just so surprised, Jack." Then like a star struck dummy I let him slip this gigantic diamond onto my finger, and worse yet I let him whisk me away to Vegas (a three hour drive) to get married in the chapel where Joan Collins married husband number four.

Now three days later, and incidentally it has been a wonderful three days except for the afternoon when I beat Jack at racquetball and he broke his racket against the wall in anger, Jack has just stopped by my desk at the library to tell me that he has arranged for us to take our upcoming three day weekend in Aruba.

Dare I go?

Sincerely,

MADLY IN LOVE WITH JACK BUT SCARED OF HIM

Dear Madly,

I don't know exactly what to tell you. The stakes are rather high. Obviously you're afraid that your husband is a serial murderer who specializes in wives.

My guess is that if the library profession were to produce a bigtime psychopathic wife murderer such a person would come out of the ranks of the catalogers. All those commas, colons, and semi-colons to be responsible for would certainly drive me to homicide. But your husband by all appearances is a well adjusted on-line searcher with some unusual insights into God. Who on earth could be trusted more than Jack?

Just the same I'm concerned about the mathematical implausibility of losing two wives to drownings. Mathematics may not be useful in proving the existence of God, but it certainly has relevance in actuarial matters. Therefore as a precaution I wouldn't make it a practice of beating Jack at racquetball, and I certainly wouldn't go near the water on your trip to Aruba. Stay on the beach and get a nice tan.

However, there is another way to look at the situation. If the first two wives did in fact die accidentally, the mathematical laws of probability dictate that the chances of your premature death (especially by drowning) are astronomically low.

Regards,
Will

P.S. Please consider including me in your will.

Spend Your Next A.L.A. Conference at the Children's Desk

Dear Will,

I am a public library director and I have been in the library profession for over fifteen years. During that time I have very dutifully attended state, regional, and national library conferences on a regular basis.

Three years ago at my state library conference in Buffalo I found myself all alone at two in the morning in the lounge of the conference hotel drinking a vodka martini and listening to the woman at the piano bar give a perfectly lovely rendition of "Stormy Weather." Upon reflection, I sadly realized that this solitary yet somewhat epiphanous experience was the highlight of my conference.

All the programs I attended were of no practical value to me or my library. In fact, Will, your own speech, although more entertaining than most, was utterly devoid of relevance to my professional life. Frothy might be a good way to describe what you had to say.

The conference exhibits were no better–just a bunch of glad-handing vendors trying to sell me stuff I either didn't want, didn't understand, or couldn't afford. I further realized that in six months I would remember only two things about this conference: (1) the stripper–Candy Lace–who mistakenly showed up at the Library Technology Roundtable Hospitality Suite on Monday evening (she thought it was the Beer Distributors meeting) and (2) Bertha Benton Jones falling down the grand central staircase of the hotel on Tuesday morning.

And in a year I'll probably only remember Bertha falling down (broken clavicle, broken pelvis). The stripper will be long forgotten by then because of the fact that a bunch of catalogers from the western part of the state stopped her in the middle of her thing and directed her to the location of the beer distributors. It was very frustrating–like watching a movie and having the projector break in the middle. I did follow Miss Lace to the Beer Convention but they had a bouncer there who refused to recognize my library association badge.

Anyway, while I was sitting there at the piano bar feeling so reflective I made a conscious decision to change my life. I decided I would no longer go to any more programs, speeches, or exhibits. The older you get, Will, the less willing you are to waste your time.

So during the last three years, while I have continued to attend library conferences, I have mainly used these trips as an opportunity to do some serious sightseeing and restaurant hopping. In the past it always frustrated me to see the detailed restaurant and tour guides published by LJ before each A.L.A. conference because I knew that the only sights I would see would be the view from my hotel window and the only restaurant I would patronize would be the hotel coffee shop. Now I can usually hit 90 to 95 percent of the restaurants on the LJ list.

Here's my problem: I've never been happier, but I've never felt guiltier. It is, after all, taxpayers' money that I am spending.

Sincerely,
HAPPY BUT GUILTY

Dear Happy,

It has never ceased to amaze me that people attend my library conference programs. Personally I wouldn't be caught dead at my speech or anyone else's. I stopped going to library conferences seven years ago. For one thing I don't sleep well in hotel rooms, and for another I sleep all too well during the conference programs.

This is not to say that the idea of library conferences is a bad one. Conferences are good for our mental health. Contrary to public opinion, we librarians do not lead the easiest lives in the world. We are chronically underpaid, overworked, understaffed, and over-stressed. We need to get away from the strain of our workaday worlds just as much as the beer distributors do.

Conferences exist to provide an opportunity to the front line librarian to back away from the daily chaos of unruly skinheads and unreasonable parents and try to get a fresh perspective on what it is that we are all about. Just mixing and mingling with librarians from other cities and states in the coffee shops and cocktail lounges of the conference hotel can sometimes be more valuable than attending a meeting on national information policy.

Library directors and library boards who require conference at-tendees to submit written reports of conference programs should be shot. Conferences should be informal and fun. Here, then, is my ad-vice: If all you are doing is waiting for your next meal, you are quite definitely wasting taxpayers' money. So instead of going to the next conference you should send one of your children's librarians in your place. She will desperately need and greatly appreciate the break from daily routine. But that's not all. While she is gone you should take her place at the children's desk.

This course of action will give you both a much needed fresh perspective.

Regards,
Will

*   *   *

Don't Ask a Fat Woman When She's Going to Have a Baby

Dear Will,

In the past five years I have worked as a reference librarian in two different libraries, and each library had a radically different philosophy of service. In the first library we were supposed to be friendly, personable, and on a first name basis with our patrons. In the second library we were instructed to be professional, business-like, and impersonal.

Which approach do you think is better?

Sincerely,
HANNAH

Dear Hannah,

There is a definite relationship between size and friendliness. The smaller the library, the friendlier you should be. People who decide to live in smaller communities expect to be treated in a warm and friendly manner and appreciate being called by their first name. In a larger city, however, many people would interpret an overly per-sonable approach in the wrong way. It's better and safer to maintain a professional distance in the urban environment. That's not to say that you can't overdo it in the small town. I can remember once striking up a conversation with a rather large patron and asking her when she was going to have her baby. "I'm not pregnant," was her icy response.

Regards,
Will

* * *

Don't Wear an Orange Tie with Red Armadillos and Expect to Be Taken Seriously

Dear Will,

When I catalog and classify the things that I don't like about civilization, ties are right at the top of my list, above oil slicks, acid rain, and sneakers with velcro straps.

Ties make no logical sense. They do not make you think better or speak more clearly. On the contrary, by restricting the flow of blood to the brain they actually impede a person's mental faculties. To make matters worse they are not inexpensive. What could be more ridiculous than paying for the opportunity to restrict the flow of blood to your brain?

Ordinarily I don't get very worked up about the subject of neckware since I haven't worn a tie for decades, but this morning on the staff room bulletin board there was a memo from my library director announcing a new dress code that requires all males on staff to wear ties and all females to wear pantyhose. "We are moving into a new library building in two weeks," the memo said, "and we all want to look worthy of our new facility."

This is just another in a long line of senseless decisions from a library director whose management style can best be described as "early monarchy." Her most salient characteristic is her rather unfortunate tendency to make an ass of herself by issuing arbitrary edicts from on high without consulting the staff.

One of the highlights of her administrative career occurred two years ago when she ordered the American flag that flies in front of our library to be lowered to half staff in honor of our janitor, Lubie, shortly after he stalled at a railroad crossing and was run over by an oncoming train. Although Lubie was beloved by all in a village idiot sort of way, the decision to fly the flag at half mast in his memory did not sit well with the mayor, the city council, and five or six hundred other citizens. We finally had to take the phone off the hook.

The whole fiasco could have been avoided of course if Linda had only paid attention to those of us on the reference staff who showed

her the presidential proclamation from the *Federal Register* specifying that the American flag can only be lowered to half mast at the command of high government officials like presidents, vice presidents, and governors. "The Proclamation says nothing about library directors," I said to Linda. She looked at me angrily and said, "Nobody but a bunch of anal retentive reference librarians cares about that kind of technical stuff!"

And now she has exacerbated her unpopularity with the staff by requiring us to wear ties and pantyhose. By putting that noose around her neck and legs she is obviously trying to tell us in a very

symbolic way that she controls us. Well we've got a big surprise in
store for her. We have all decided to get even with her by wearing
the funkiest, most outlandish neckware and legware imaginable for
her precious Grand Opening.

How does an orange tie decorated with red armadillos grab you?

Sincerely,
A WILD AND CRAZY REFERENCE LIBRARIAN

Dear Wild,

If you wore that to my Grand Opening I'd strangle you with it.
What is wrong with the concept of showing up to work looking
halfway fashionable? Librarians are always complaining about their
nerdy image and yet are seemingly brain damaged when it comes to
understanding why the image exists. To be taken seriously you have
to dress seriously, unless of course you're Albert Einstein.

Since you're obviously not Albert Einstein I'd suggest that you
do yourself a favor and look in the mirror. I'm confident that will be
all the motivation you will need to go out and get a new wardrobe.
Maybe then your director will give you the attention that you so obviously desire.

Best Regards,
Will

Every Library Director Needs an Occasional Swift Kick of Reality

Dear Will,

I am the head of circulation for a public library. Let me be fair
about our new library director. He is an honest man. He is a literate
man. He is a nice man. But he does have a fatal flaw. He gives too
much credence to the people who call him up to register complaints
about the library.

Whatever the caller says becomes gospel to Mr. K. If, for

instance, someone were to call him and tell him that I shot and killed a library patron who complained about a fine, the first thing Mr. K. would do would be to call the police and have me arrested. He works on a "guilty until proven innocent" philosophy.

Instead of supporting the circ staff, he is continually putting us in a defensive posture. It gets to the point where we have to justify everything we do. As a result we now routinely allow our more vocal (and obnoxious) patrons to break every rule they want to break. Letting them get away with murder is preferable to having them call up Mr. K. to get us in trouble.

Any suggestions that you might have regarding how we can get Mr. K. to support us rather than our crackpot patrons would be greatly appreciated.

Sincerely,

DESPERATE

Dear Desperate,

This is a tough one, Mr. K. obviously wants to establish the fact that he is an effective public administrator who is responsible to the taxpaying public.

Your strategy of "giving the store away" everytime someone threatens to call Mr. K. only makes matters worse. Pretty soon you will lose all credibility and authority in the eyes of your patrons and you will be unable to enforce any of your circulation rules or regulations.

The best way to solve Mr. K's lack of confidence in the staff is to start sending your problem patrons up to see him whenever they have a gripe. Two things will happen very quickly. First, Mr. K will see these people as the deadbeats and con artists that they really

are, and second, Mr. K. will get so tired of seeing these malcontents
in his office that he will never criticize his circ staff again.

Circ staffers have the most difficult job in the library. They get
none of the warm fuzzies that reference and children's librarians get
from their users. A supportive director, therefore, is a necessity.

Regards,
Will

There Are No Laws Against Stupidity

Dear Will,

I am a reference librarian in a large urban public library and I
am concerned about a possible conflict-of-interest issue that has
recently arisen in my work.

There is a man named Elmer T. who uses the library frequently,
and I have helped him on many occasions. He is an amateur inven-
tor. Actually that's not quite right. Inventing is Elmer's occupation;
he just hasn't made any money from it. But he is on the verge of a
major breakthrough.

Elmer T. has invented an exercise machine that you use while
you are asleep. It is a pedal contraption that you strap your feet into
when you go to bed. Then you set the timer. If you are a fast sleeper
you would set the timer for fifteen minutes; if you are a tosser and a
turner you might set the timer for one hour.

When the timer goes off the machine is activated. The pedals do
all the work. They move your legs up and down while you are sleep-
ing. The concept of the machine is brilliant because it does away
with the two things that keep most people from exercising – pain and
boredom.

I know that this new device (tentatively called "The Sleepcycle")
will make millions for Elmer. Because I have been so helpful to him
at the library, he has offered me the opportunity to invest in his

machine. Lord knows as a librarian I can use the money that will no doubt come rolling in as soon as the Sleepcycle is marketed, but I don't want to profit illegally from the inside information that I have gotten by virtue of my work as a public employee.

Am I violating any legal, ethical, or professional standards?

Sincerely,

RICHARD AND SOON TO BE RICH

Dear Rich,

The only standard you are violating is the standard of intelligence. Are you for real? Even if this thing works, it will have

absolutely no aerobic value. You'd be better off investing in
checkered paint.

Regards,
Will

Adolf Hitler Was Single,
but So Was Jesus Christ

Dear Will,

I know that unless you want to get sued you should never ask
personal questions of a job candidate. However, based on twenty-five
years of experience, I have decided that information about a candidate's personal life is very important in making a hiring decision.

Specifically, I have a  theory that married
people with children make the best employees
and that single people without children make
the worst. Married people without children fall
somewhere in between. Single people are too self-absorbed Everything
is a crisis for them, and since they have no one else in their life their
job tends to become an obsession, which drives all their co-workers
up a wall. They tend to be workaholics, and they just don't understand those of us who have family responsibilities and therefore can't
work 23-hour days. Hitler was single, and so was Charles Manson.

Married people with children, on the other hand, are forced by
the necessity of being part of a family to become good communi-
cators. They relate well to other employees and know how to keep
disturbances, like screaming children, in perspective.

Married people without children are okay to talk to, but they
tend to be rather spoiled. Have you ever seen an adult couple dining
at McDonald's without children? Of course not. That's my point. They
tend to think life is just one big ethnic restaurant.

The smart library administrator will therefore break the law and
use any means necessary to determine the marital and family status
of all job candidates.

Sincerely,
RHODA

Dear Rhoda,

Your theory is fascinating. I just have one question. If married people are so cooperative, why are there so many divorces?

Regards,
Will

P.S. I'm married with three children and everytime I hear a child scream in the library I want to get out my deer rifle.

Plumbers Eat Donuts; Librarians Eat Pastries

Dear Will,

I've been in the library administration business for over thirty years and obviously in that time I've lived through an awful lot of changes. For instance, thirty years ago you could "host" a meeting without providing food, but today you can't. Today everyone expects to be fed.

It seems that staff meetings, board meetings, committee meetings, and library association meetings cannot be held without calling in a caterer. Don't people eat at home anymore?

Six months ago it was my turn to host the regular monthly meeting of our regional council of library directors. I set up the conference room, put on a pot of coffee, and gave a warm welcoming speech as soon as everyone had arrived. The meeting, however, went poorly. Everyone seemed to be testier than usual, and very little business was conducted.

I sulked about this for several weeks, and then finally a close colleague of mine from a neighboring city called and confided to me that the other directors were unhappy because "appropriate snacks" had not been provided. Obviously they felt slighted.

Last Friday it was again my turn to host the monthly meeting. This time I was prepared or so I thought. I sent my secretary out to one of those drive-up doughnut chains to buy an assortment of not one, not two, but three dozen doughnuts for the meeting.

To my great dismay, however, things again did not go well. During the course of our three hour meeting only four doughnuts were eaten, all by Agnes Armstrong Bartles who weighs more than 200 pounds. She also put three doughnuts in the pockets of her raincoat as she was leaving.

Will, what am I doing wrong?

Sincerely,
HUNGRY FOR ADVICE

Dear Hungry,

Like you, I find the new phenomenon of "you can't have a meeting without food" to be greatly regrettable. Be assured, however, that it is not just an idiosyncrasy of the library profession. Just yesterday I read an article that stated that the special congressional taskforce appointed to reduce the federal budget spent $60,000 on food in just ten days. That's the main reason why I am against serving food at meetings – it's a frivolous use of taxpayers' money.

It also stretches meetings out unnecessarily. People, librarians included, tend to hunker down and settle in on a full stomach. Most library meetings are full of hot air signifying nothing. If anything they should be shortened, not prolonged.

But my complaints don't help you. Librarians expect not only to be fed but to be fed appropriately. Your mistake with the doughnuts is an obvious one. Drive-up doughnut chains specialize in cheap doughy doughnuts that stick to your fingers, gum up your dental work, and drip on your tie. A cheap doughnut is the last thing you want to handle when you are all dressed up for a meeting. No wonder that no one but Agnes Armstrong Bartles ate them.

Although we librarians do not make a lot of money, we do have expensive tastes. We appreciate the finer things in life. Therefore the next time you're asked to host a morning meeting, seek out a quality bakery and buy an eclectic assortment of dainty ethnic pastries that are easy to handle and even easier to eat. Librarians love foods with foreign names.

The smaller the pastries the better off you'll be. People will eat little pastries because they think that they can control their caloric intake that way. Of course, that is an illusion. I have seen librarians who will not touch a single glazed doughnut eat seven little French tarts in less than ten minutes.

Follow this advice and I guarantee you'll regain your professional respect in no time.

> Regards,
> Will

*　　*　　*

Don't Put Up Mistletoe If You Don't Want Anyone to Be Kissed

Dear Will,

There is a word in the English language – "appropriate" – that is rather difficult to define but which most people understand instinctively. It means if you are a reference librarian you don't put the university president on hold; it means that if you are a children's librarian you don't tell the chair of the board of trustees that his daughter cannot participate in story hour because all sessions are filled; and it means that if you are an acquisitions librarian that you don't tell a city councilman that you won't order the book he wants because it hasn't gotten two positive reviews.

My twenty years of public library experience have taught me that most staffers know instinctively what actions are appropriate for a given situation and what actions are not appropriate. For that reason I have never believed in handing down a lot of personnel rules and regulations from on high. A dress code is a good example of an unnecessary policy. Why should I try to dictate what my employees wear when I know that 95 percent of them will dress appropriately without any advice from me? It has always been my very strong opinion that if you treat library employees as responsible adults they will act like responsible adults, and if you treat them as children, they will act like children.

Last week, however, something happened that has raised questions about my view that you can expect your librarians to behave in an appropriate fashion. Specifically, Eleanor, our nonfiction cataloging specialist, showed up at the annual staff/board Christmas party (which I always host in my home) in a tight red dress with a neckline that plunged down to the waistline and with a hemline that rose up to the region of the upper thigh.

To my great chagrin, Eleanor, who has never been known to dress provocatively, became the centerpiece of attention at *my* party.

The richly diverse smorgasbord of finger snadwiches and pastries that I slaved so diligently over was largely neglected, and the festive garlands of holly, the antique ornaments, and the brightly colored pine cones that adorned my house were for the most part unnoticed. Even the roaring and crackling fire of oak and maple logs in the living room hearth played second fiddle to Eleanor's damn red dress. The only holiday decoration that attracted any attention was the mistletoe that I hung from the family room ceiling, and that's only because Eleanor spent most of her time under it being kissed. And then, God forbid, some of my partiers started moving my furniture around to create a makeshift dance floor, and worse yet they put some of my 15-year-old son's rock records on the stereo for their dance music. What an abomination!

Eleanor is newly divorced, but really did she have to make her recent availability so obvious? Besides the resentment I feel about her turning my party into a meat market, I am very concerned about the impact that her dress will have on the way the Board views the library staff.

My question is, do you think it is appropriate for me to put out a dress code governing what is and is not appropriate to wear at library social functions?

Sincerely,
LOUISE

Dear Louise,

Your Christmas party sounds like it was far too festive. Library social events are supposed to be boring, nerve-racking affairs where the main activity is sitting in a corner and watching the onion dip turn green. Dancing at a library party is indeed an abomination, and kissing under the mistletoe is not only obscene but also unsafe in this age of AIDS. By all means you need to put out a dress code to prevent anybody from having any fun in the future.

Bah Humbug,
Will

*   *   *

A No Limit Check-Out Policy Makes Weeding Unnecessary

Dear Will,

I hate rules. I hate forms. I hate red tape. I hate uniformity. Why I got into librarianship I'm not quite sure. One look at AACR2 gives me intense existential nausea. My main motivation in becoming a director was to put myself in a position where I could arbitrarily do away with all the petty rules that give our profession a bad name.

This decision was very popular with the public but it did not sit well with my circulation staff. They told me I was making a huge

mistake when I abolished the limit of books that a patron can check out at any one time. They said that under my no-limit policy one patron could theoretically check out the entire collection. I responded by saying that the problem with circulation clerks is that they are pessimists who stay up at night thinking about everything that can go wrong in life.

As things turned out I grudgingly have to admit that my circ people may have been right.

Two weeks ago they reported to me that an overweight man with a scar on his right cheek checked out 303 books off the bookmobile, and then last week he checked out a total of 417 books from various branches in our system. But that's not all. Yesterday he checked out 79 books from main. That means he now has a grand total of 799 library books in his possession.

What do you suppose he's doing with all those books?

Sincerely,
WORRIED

Dear Worried,

My guess is that he is either working on a doctoral dissertation or selling your books to a used book dealer. Take your pick.

Regards,
Will

It's Too Bad a Breast Enhancement Operation Does Nothing for the Brain

Dear Will,

I'm a library assistant (circulation department) and I'm having a major problem with my library director. He doesn't think that the breast enhancement surgery that I have planned for next month is covered under what he calls "our self-insured medical program." He says, "Our medical policy is intended for legitimate illnesses only," and I go, "Hey, it's not like I'm having my tummy tucked or my chin lifted." Then he says, "Sorry, your problem is not an illness," and I go, "What do you want me to do—get wired on coke like Janie in cataloging and have my six week vacation at the rehab center paid in full by our self-insured medical program?" He says, "Case closed; you do not have a legitimate medical need," and I go, "I call it serious when your boyfriend threatens to leave you if you don't get implants plus it will improve my appearance at the circ desk." Then he just turns his back on me and walks away. I'm like I can't believe this is happening to me.

Sincerely,
ALISON

Dear Alison,

Forget the breast enhancement and schedule some brain surgery.

Regards,
Will

What's Good for General Motors Is Good for the Public Library

Dear Will,

My director, Mr. Fredericks, is positively passionate about the importance of public libraries to the future of America. He thinks that the public library, which he calls the University of the People, is the last free educational institution of higher learning for the common man. "Strong libraries are just as important to a democracy as strong armies," is his favorite quote. Obviously librarianship to him is not just a profession; it is a crusade.

As with a lot of crusaders, Mr. Fredericks does not entirely understand those of us on staff (I am a reference librarian) who enjoy going to work every day but who also enjoy going home at night. Librarianship for us is strictly an eight hour a day proposition, a nice way to earn a living and pay the bills. We reserve our passion for other things like collecting old buttons and jumping out of airplanes.

For Mr. Fredericks, however, librarianship is a 24-hour obligation. He feels that as professionals we should be committed to fighting for libraries in the political arena. This means that he expects us to lobby for library legislation and support and work for political candidates who are library advocates.

Although no one has ever been penalized for not "getting committed," it is very clear that promotions and raises go to those who in Mr. Fredericks' words "make the extra effort on behalf of a noble profession."

I am very troubled by this because I do not think it is fair. I am as good a reference librarian as you will find anywhere but I can't seem to get any recognition from Mr. Fredericks because I don't participate in his little political crusades and I absolutely refuse to wear political buttons while working.

Also I am somewhat bothered by the fact that all of Mr. Fredericks' favored candidates seem to be Democrats. It makes me wonder if he is more interested in supporting Democrats than in supporting libraries.

Sincerely,
SUSAN

Dear Susan,

You have a very legitimate concern. Mr. Fredericks is way out of line in putting pressure on you and the rest of the staff to get political on your time off for several reasons. First, you owe him eight hours and that is all. It is completely inappropriate for him, on

ethical and legal grounds, to try to dictate what you should do with your free time. That's why we have labor laws – to protect workers from unfair labor practices. You should tell Fredericks that the fight for the eight hour work day was won decades and decades ago and how would he like to go to court to resolve the matter.

Also there is a practical issue here. Librarians should forget about their work when they are off duty to prevent the unfortunate effects of stress and burnout. You'll be a much better reference librarian if you spend your free time collecting old buttons and jumping out of airplanes.

To further compound the problem, as a public official it is unlawful for Fredericks to pressure his employees into political action. This too is a right that governmental workers won a long time ago. Perhaps you should introduce your director to the twentieth century.

Finally, Fredericks makes a common mistake. He falsely assumes that public libraries benefit more from the election of Democratic candidates than Republicans. The fact of the matter is that more than anything public libraries benefit from a healthy economy. When the economy is strong, our tax base is strong. When the economy is weak, our tax base is weak. The candidates who do the most to help private companies, do the most to help public libraries. It's as simple as that.

Therefore you should always vote for the candidate who you think will be most effective at stimulating the economy. Party labels and public advocacy of libraries have nothing to do with that. Just look at Jimmy Carter, a big library advocate and a former library board member, whose economic policies set back public libraries in this country for years. Ronald Reagan, on the other hand, was not a big library supporter, but because the economy flourished under his eight year reign, public libraries flourished also.

Sincerely,
Will

*   *   *

Molesworth Members Have More Fun

Dear Will,

I am a library school student anxious to make my mark in the profession. What, in your opinion, is the greatest professional honor that a librarian can aspire to – winning the Isadore Gilbert Mudge  Award, being elected president of the American Library Association, becoming director of the Harvard Library, winning the deanship of the Berkeley Library School, getting your picture on the cover of Library Journal, being appointed Librarian of Congress, or earning a six figure salary with an automobile allowance?

> Sincerely,
> CEDRIC

Dear Cedric,

None of those honors impress me. When I get a résumé from a job-seeker the first thing I do is look for membership in the Molesworth Institute – there is no greater honor in our profession.

> Regards,
> Will (a member of the Molesworth Institute)

When You Chain a Pen You Invite Violence

Dear Will,

Is it the responsibility of the library to provide patrons with scratch paper and golf pencils at the public access terminals and at the magazine index tables?

My janitor is very tired of finding scratch paper all over the floor, and I am very tired of losing literally hundreds of golf pencils to thoughtless and dishonest patrons who walk off with them. Golf pencils are not cheap. A two pound box, which lasts one day if we are lucky, costs almost $10.

Do you think we should do what the banks do and fasten chained pens to our on-line catalogs? I never thought I would do this, but our golf pencils keep disappearing at an alarming rate. We have tried signs – DO NOT REMOVE PENCILS – but they are ignored.

Sincerely,
AT WIT'S END

Dear Wit,

First, about the scratch paper. Are you going to let your janitor run the library? It happens to be his job to clean the floors. If he had his way, you would never open your doors to the public. Of course you should make scratch paper available to your patrons.

Second, DO NOT DO WHAT THE BANKS DO! NEVER CHAIN A PEN TO YOUR ONLINE CARELS OR YOUR INDEX TABLES. NEVER. Chained pens give only a limited amount of slack (usually five to eight inches). THERE IS NOTHING MORE MADDENING IN THIS WORLD THAN TRYING TO WRITE WITH A CHAINED PEN. YOU ALWAYS RUN OUT OF CHAIN. When this happens, people get very hostile and they angrily try to rip the pen right out of the desk that it's attached to. Many beautiful pieces of library furniture have been ruined this way.

I once saw a man (he must have been an electrician) get so mad at a chained pen that he went out to his truck, got a pair of wire cutters, came back, and cut the chain in two. It goes against our nature to chain anything. We human beings love our freedom and our mobility. Anyone who chains a pen to a desk has to be willing to pay the price. Stick with the golf pencils. They're not a perfect solution, but we don't live in a perfect world.

Regards,
Will

You Can Run Away from Your Past

Dear Will,

This dilemma is purely my fault. For years I cultivated the image of the happy-go-lucky, devil-take-the-hindmost, free-wheeling, free drinking, fun-time guy. My life was a beer commercial. I was always the first to get to happy hour after work and the last to leave. At library conventions I was the eternal life of the party, and my hotel room was party headquarters. For close to eight years "King of the Party Beasts" was my unofficial title at the college library where I worked. My one mission in life was to singlehandedly destroy the image of the librarian as a stern and morally upright taskmaster. I thought that this was a noble undertaking.

And then one morning I woke up sick on somebody's lawn and stared into the great chasm of death. I was 31 years old and terrified of the future. That morning marked the beginning of the end of my drunkenness and debauchery. My conversion to Christianity, however, was not the explosive and immediate miracle that St. Paul experienced on the road to Damascus. My arrival in the house of God was a slow and tortuous journey filled with minor victories and major defeats. There were some months when I was convinced that God did not even know that I was alive, and other months when I felt he was watching my every move.

Throughout this journey I continued to drink and to party, but gradually the light of the true way began to outshine the darkness of my debauchery. Now four years after my initial terror of death, I consider myself to be healed.

But unfortunately my past haunts me. My colleagues sense that something has happened to me mentally, emotionally, and spiritually, but they're just not sure what it is. I think they miss the old me – the life of the party, the purveyor of fun. They continue, therefore, to treat me like a Neanderthal in a beer commercial. Besides being personally offended by this treatment, I am growing worried about my image. I have worked as a reference librarian in the same university library for 12 years without a promotion. I think my career has stalled because of my wild reputation.

What has really upset me is that this past Christmas my colleagues at the library gave me bottles of gin, rum, and vodka for my Christmas presents. I now have enough liquor to open up a tavern, but I haven't taken a drop of alcohol for over 11 months, not one drop. I am thoroughly depressed. My friends obviously don't take my conversion seriously. They are ridiculing me.

What should I do?

> Sincerely,
> NICK

Dear Nick,

This is very easy. You need to flee your past. You need a change of scenery and a fresh start. Dust off your résumé and start over in a library where no one knows about your past or your reputation. Do this even if it means a cut in pay. If you stay where you are there's a good chance you'll start drinking again.

> Sincerely,
> Will

Even Jesus Christ Was Not Perfect When It Came to Hiring the Apostles

Dear Will,

I am the supervisor of a 10-person cataloging department in a university library. One of my strengths, at least that's what everyone tells me, is that I am a very good judge of talent and character. I seem to have a sixth sense for picking out the perfect person for openings in my department, and I have to admit that my track record is flawless.

Of all the people I have hired over the past 12 years I have only had to discharge one—the man that I selected as our Romance language specialist. It turned out he was even better in the romance area than I had anticipated. We fell in love and got married. Under university policy he could no longer work for me after the wedding, which was just fine since that freed him up to stay home with the three children that we eventually had. So you see, I do have impeccable taste.

But now I am faced with a situation that quite frankly has me rather baffled. Two months ago my Slavic languages cataloger

retired after 30 years of excellent service. I begged her to stay on but she had her heart set on a little trailer park in Coral Gables, Florida (I understand there's a whole colony of retired catalogers living there).

As you probably know, Slavic language cataloging specialists do not grow on trees, but I got lucky. One of my applicants not only had an excellent academic background in the field but also spent three years working in Slavic at the Library of Congress.

Yesterday I called her to offer her the job. She was not immediately available and so I was put on hold. While holding, I happened to scan through her job application one more time and noticed that under the heading of "Organizations" she had put the letters "A.A." This, of course, gave me a sudden jolt. Certainly she had meant to put "A.L.A." down. She couldn't possibly have meant A.A. When she finally came to the phone, instead of offering her the job, I asked her if the A.A. was a typo. "Oh no," she said, "it stands for Alcoholics Anonymous." Then after an uncomfortable pause, she said very forthrightly, "I am an alcoholic, but I've been sober for eighteen months."

Now I didn't know what to do. This woman was definitely the best qualified person for the job. But I'm just not sure that I want to take the risk that she'll start drinking again. My big regret is that she put "A.A." down on her application in the first place. If she hadn't, she would have a job now and I would be able to sleep at night.

The way I analyze it is that now that I know that she is in A.A., I have to take direct responsibility for her behavior. If I do hire her and she does start drinking again, then I can be reprimanded for knowingly hiring an alcoholic.

What should I do?

Sincerely,
IGNORANCE IS BLISS

Dear Bliss,

By all means hire the woman. The bottom line, as you freely admit, is that Slavic language cataloging specialists do not grow on trees. Alcoholism, although a serious disease, is not the same sort of psychosis that rapists and murderers suffer from. This woman is not a threat to anyone's safety or health.

The only thing that you are endangering by hiring this woman is your own "flawless track record." Your biggest fear seems to be that this woman might be your first hiring mistake. Don't worry about that. Everyone makes hiring mistakes. Even Jesus Chris was wrong about Judas.

So lighten up. This woman is at least honest. Would you really have preferred a closet drinker? My prediction is that your Slavic cataloging will be better than ever even with old what'shername packing it off to the Florida trailer park.

But, I might be very wrong. This woman could start drinking at anytime. That's what makes personnel management a challenge.

Regards,
Will

P.S. Judging by the amount of drinking that goes on at A.L.A. conferences, maybe you're better off with an A.A. member than an A.L.A. member.

Fat Men Who Pick Up Lawn Mowers Should Not Wear Blue Underpants

Dear Will,

Yesterday morning before work I took my lawn mower (a top of the line, five-blade reel model with six different height settings) to the repair shop to be tuned up and sharpened.

If someone had directed a video camera at me as I lifted the mower out of the truck of my Honda hatchback the resulting footage would have been fodder for a television blooper show because my pants split neatly and cleanly with the effect of exposing my powder blue underpants to the world. In case you've never had this experience the sense of nakedness that you feel is considerable.

Unwilling to reveal more of my underpants to the universe, I promptly wrestled the mower back into the hatchback and headed directly home to change my pants. As a result I got to my job at the reference desk of the local public library 45 minutes late. Like any responsible employee I had been thoughtful enough to call ahead and inform my supervisor, Sally, that I was going to be late due to the fact that I had ripped my pants in a most embarrassing place.

I knew that Sally would be upset because my tardiness meant that she would actually have to do some real work filling in for me. Sally is the type of supervisor who prefers to spend her mornings leafing through library journals and drinking coffee. Consequently when I finally did arrive at the desk, I apologized profusely. This did not help. She was indeed in a bad mood and instead of allowing me to make up the time by skipping my lunch break, she docked me a whole hour of vacation time!

I think this is completely unfair, but she claims that since my accident did not occur at work it would be inappropriate for me to have the opportunity to make up the time.

How do you feel?

Sincerely,
RONALD

Dear Ronald,

I think that the problem is even more basic than where and how you split your pants. Have you ever considered the possibility that your pants are too tight or that you are too fat?

Go run around the block a few times and lose some weight. If you don't want to do that at least buy some white underpants.

Regards,
Will

*   *   *

Doodling Nudes Is Quite Different from Doodling Nude

Dear Will,

Please let's keep this one anonymous, shall we? I am a defender of intellectual freedom and am somewhat embarrassed by the nature of my problem.

As the head of reference in a university library, I have a meeting with my librarians every other Wednesday to talk about common problems, discuss policy changes, and review new acquisitions. In my opinion these meetings are not oppressively long. They take anywhere from 45 minutes to an hour.

Fred is one of my ten reference librarians, and he is a doodler on a rather grand scale. Where some doodlers will doodle away discreetly on a hidden corner of their notepad, Fred gets so engrossed in his doodling that he does nothing to hide his doodles. To me the expert doodler is the person who can produce a series of interesting doodles while creating the impression that he or she is actually taking notes.

Fred, however, makes no effort to conceal his doodling. From the standpoint of running a meeting this can be very distracting, doubly so when you consider what kinds of things Fred likes to doodle. The librarians inevitably let their eyes wander away from me and towards Fred's doodles. It is not so much that Fred is the world's greatest doodler, it's just that his subject matter is so arresting.

Fred doodles nudes – large, rather overstated nudes of both genders. The only way I could compete with that is by getting on the conference room table and doing a striptease.

In summary I find his doodling to be most rude, and I'd like to ban it or at least restrict his subject matter to less captivating forms and figures. I hesitate to do this for fear of being ridiculed unmercifully by the staff for violating Fred's rights of intellectual freedom.

Do you feel that Fred's doodling is protected by the First Amendment?

Sincerely,
ZONA

Dear Zona,

From the tone of your letter you would think that Fred was not just doodling nudes, but also doodling in the nude.

When will uptight supervisors like you ever learn that you cannot simply dictate the thoughts and actions of your employees. Instead of censoring his doodling why not just require him to get a lobotomy?

Has it ever occurred to you that people doodle when they are bored, and that they doodle nudes when they are bored out of their skulls? Perhaps before you start making noises about infringing on Fred's First Amendment rights you should think about streamlining your meetings or eliminating them altogether.

If you can't compete with a doodler that doesn't say much about your ability as a communicator, does it? Have you ever thought about joining Toastmasters?

Sincerely,
Will

P.S. The nude is a classical form that has challenged the masters for ages. Be flattered that as long as your doodler is wasting time he is doing it in a grandiose fashion.

Do Not Force Your Employees to Leave Their Kids with Mass Murderers

Dear Will,

I am the director of a medium sized public library and there is no one I feel more sympathetic to than the single parent. In fact I am a single mother. I have a daughter in junior high school and no husband. He left me last year. At the time he left he said he needed his "space." His "space" turned out to be a younger woman – my daughter's math teacher.

I suppose it was my fault in a way. Ordinarily I attend all of my daughter's parent-teacher conferences but last year I couldn't because of a conflict with a library board meeting. So my husband went instead, and obviously sparks flew.

Actually this doesn't bother me as much as you would think. My husband was not the greatest thing since the microwave oven. In fact, he had certain disgusting personal habits with regards to his toes and toenails that I quite thankfully no longer have to endure. Ironically, I'm the one enjoying space. After 13 years of picking up after him, I can breathe again. My daughter and I are best friends.

But I know that if my daughter were younger I'd be in a much bigger pickle. Child care is a horrendous problem for single mothers who work in libraries, and 40 percent of our library staff are single mothers. They have gone through a sadly similar series of events – marriage, children, abuse, and abandonment. In some of these cases the weight of dependent responsibilities has been further burdened by the recent arrival of a frail or elderly parent. Don't men do anything anymore?

Since libraries are open all hours of the day and night as well as on weekdays and weekends, our single mothers are in a real bind. Finding childcare at night or on Saturday or Sunday is much like playing Russian roulette. As one of my circ clerks put it, "You can either quit your job and go on welfare or you can leave your child with some old lady who may or may not be a mass murderer." There is, of course, one other option. You can dump your kid in the library and hope that he or she will sit still with a book and blend unobtrusively into the furniture for four hours.

My immediate problem involves an employee who leaves her four year old in the children's room while she works circulation. Like most children that age, this boy cannot sit still for more than thirty seconds. He is physically and verbally disruptive. The children's librarians spend half their time trying to keep him under control.

I know that I must tell the circ clerk to make other arrangements but I don't want to force her to quit her job, and I don't want her to leave her child with a mass murderer. Is this why administrators make more money?

Sincerely,
FEELING VERY GUILTY

Dear Guilty,

Child care is the biggest problem in America today. It is bigger than drug abuse, bigger than the budget deficit, and bigger than the plight of the woodland owl. It is the problem from which all other social problems stem.

Fifteen years ago, I would have given you the cold-hearted advice to can the circ clerk for having the gall to bring her child to work with her. Today, however, I advise caution and patience. Although it is not in your job description, you need to do some social work. First, temporarily adjust the circ clerk's schedule so that she works at times that the day care centers are open. Then use your community contacts to find out all the acceptable child care options available for nights and weekends. You might even suggest that all the single mothers on your staff form a support group or task force to deal with the problem.

If you go this extra mile you will be rewarded with a loyal, supportive staff appreciative of the fact that you see them as real people and not just interchangeable parts of the library bureaucracy.

Regards,
Will

Don't Try to Teach a Cat to Bark

Dear Will,

My question is a simple one. Can I evaluate my employees by the appearance of their desk?

As a mid-level supervisor, I find myself caught in the middle of a major controversy. Our new library director is demanding that every library employee maintain a clean desk. He wants the library to have a businesslike and professional image. Some of my employees have clean desks and some of them have messy desks.

The messy desk people say that a clean desk means one of two things: (1) the person has nothing to do, or (2) the person is anal retentive. The clean desk people claim that the messy desk people are sloppy, inefficient, unreliable, and disorganized. This controversy is causing a Civil War–type of atmosphere in our library. The clean desk people are constantly monitoring the work surfaces of the

messy desk people. We haven't had such a schism since smoking was banned in the staff lounge.

What are your views?

Sincerely,

WAR WEARY

Dear Weary,

First, let me put my bias on the table. I come down firmly on the side of the clean deskers. I cannot tolerate messy desks. They make me very nervous. What with earthquakes, tornadoes, hurricanes, and tidal waves, the earth is already an overly chaotic place. Must man contribute to this chaos?

There is nothing more annoying to a clean desker, like myself, than to happen upon a messy desk. It doesn't matter if I'm in a bank, a business, or a library, I compulsively start cleaning up every messy desk that I encounter. This nervous disorder of mine, which I'm sure is shared by other clean deskers, is rooted in the belief that those who cannot keep a clean desk cannot take care of the planet. I have always suspected, for example, that oil spills were caused by people with messy desks – people who were never taught by their parents to pick up their toys. If nonsmokers have a right to live in a smoke free environment, we clean deskers feel that we have a right to live in a clutter free environment.

Unfortunately for us the messy deskers are not reluctant to stand up for their rights, and their argument is indeed an interesting one: "If we can prove to be as productive as people who have clean desks, don't we have a right to keep our desk any way that we please?" It's an interesting question – does a productive employee have a right to a messy desk? Unfortunately the Constitution has nothing to say about this issue.

Personally, I had my eyes opened by a woman that I promoted to a high administrative post in my library. She is one of the best librarians that I have ever met – personable, intelligent, experienced, and very knowledgeable about all aspects of library science. Her work has always been on time and of the highest quality.

For many years it was a continuing source of irritation for me, therefore, to walk past her hopelessly messy desk which stood as a stubborn counterweight to my theory that people who have a messy desk do inferior work. After I promoted her, I insisted that she keep a clean desk as an example to the rest of the staff.

Her solemn resolve to make this effort, however, did not last long. Within days her desk was back to being a shambles. It became obvious to me that there was something in her genetic makeup that made it impossible for her to maintain a neat and tidy desk. There was no way that I could teach this cat to bark. Her work, however, was better than ever. She rose to the challenge of her new job with unsurpassed excellence.

Because of this experience I have made it a point to observe the condition of all my employees' desks and try to determine if there is in fact a correlation between desktop neatness and work performance. My findings are twofold: (1) there is no correlation, and (2) the only time that you should be concerned about the condition of a person's desk is if there is some abrupt change. For instance, if a messy desker all of a sudden gets neat or a clean desker all of a sudden gets messy, there may be some deep emotional problems at work. Keep sharp objects away from them.

> I hope this helps,
> Will

When in Doubt Think Taupe

Dear Will,

I am in the middle of the design phase of a $10 million public library building project. This is the first building design that I have been involved in, and for the most part everything has been going surprisingly well. All the architects, designers, and consultants have been great to work with.

I was dismayed, therefore, at what happened at last night's library board meeting when the members of the project design team made what was supposed to be their final presentation to the board. The main architect and engineer did well enough. For almost an hour they talked in great detail about space allocations, floor plans, exterior elevations, site amenities, building materials, and lighting levels with not one word of dissent from any of the trustees. Actually I think everybody was rather overwhelmed by the immensity of the project.

But then the interior designer got up and made his presentation. Immediately I knew we were in deep trouble. First of all, I wouldn't call our designer a tranvestive per se. Usually he looks rather androgynous in what I would call his "designer chic" outfits. You know – the baggy pants, baggy shirt, shoes that look like bedroom slippers, and a ringed earring in the left ear. Let's face it, like most creative people, he does his own unique thing appearance wise. And when you really think about it, would you want a designer to look normal? Of course not. You're interested in someone who will be at least a little bit daring and innovative. You want your library's interior to have its own special look. Therefore a good designer should have the look of an artiste.

But last night he looked absolutely feminine. He wore two earrings instead of one, and they both dangled. Plus he did something frizzy to his hair that made him look like he belonged on the cover of a Spiegel catalog. And as the topper, he wore lipstick to match the color scheme of the building – plum. Needless to say, this did not go over real big with the board members who are strictly down-the-middle type people – lawyers, insurance salesmen, concerned parents, that sort of thing. The hair and earrings were possibly tolerable, but the lip gloss was simply too much for the board to handle.

"Personally I find plum to be a perfectly repulsive color," was board member Trudy Matthews' comment. What she meant of course is that plum lipstick on a man is perfectly repulsive. Myself, I think that plum is a perfect interior color for a library. It gives you some warmth without, as my designer says, "getting in your face."

The board, of course, was completely incapable of seeing it that way. I am unable to predict the future but I am 100 percent certain that you will not find the color plum inside my new building. So what will the new color be? I have no idea. The whole situation is out of control.

Ours is a seven member board. Five of the seven are women. The two men do not care about color. They have agreed to go along with whatever colors the women settle on. The problem is that the women can't agree on anything. Trudy is into earth tones, Catherine likes the blue family, Diana prefers cheerful pastels, Paula is a purple person, and Edna wants black and white and red all over.

My designer is absolutely aghast at all of these suggestions and is threatening to quit because he has lost his artistic control of the project. On the other hand, my five ladies cannot agree, cannot even agree to disagree. It's turning into a nasty battle of egos. Trudy accuses Diana of being color blind, Paula thinks Edna is acting pretentiously, and Catherine is busy playing the expert (she claims to have taken a course in interior decoration at a local community college).

Meanwhile the project is on hold until this color war has ended. Any bright ideas?

Sincerely,
COLOR ME BLUE

Dear Blue,

First get rid of the designer. It is true that he has lost artistic control of the project but it's his own darn fault. I don't care how much of an artiste he is, any man who wears two dangling earrings and lip gloss to a library board meeting should be shot.

Second, don't despair completely. Your problem is not all that unusual. Interior colors are always controversial. Library trustees often feel very impotent in dealing with the highly technical issues that concern architects and engineers. They simply don't have the expertise to deal intelligently with the details of building design and construction. They are therefore very reluctant to say "boo" about a building's proposed structure.

But colors are an entirely different matter. Everybody is an expert on colors, and we all have our favorites. Like you say, Paula is a purple person. Personally, I like brown. Picking interior colors, is the one way that a library board can leave a lasting imprint on a library building. Trustees want to feel a part of the design process if only in this small, but not insignificant way.

What usually happens when trustees try to pick colors is exactly what is happening in your situation – friction, controversy, and in-fighting. Here's my advice: you have to come up with a miracle color, what I call a "chameleon" color, a color that everyone on the board will claim as her own. Up until last week I didn't think that such a thing existed.

Now I do. I happened to be clothes shopping, pants to be specific, and I stumbled upon a pair that appeared to be the precise shade of dirty tan that I was looking for. When I got the pants home under a different light, however, they seemed more like a member of the gray family, and in the morning sunlight they took on the tinge of a muted blue or even purple. Sometimes at night they even appear to be a bit burgundy, which is another of my favorite colors. But that's not all. I've also discovered that I can wear any tie or coat with these pants and the overall effect is quite nice, even attractive.

Curious, I went back to the store and discovered that the pants were called "taupe." The word "taupe" is even as interesting as the color. You look in one dictionary and it says "brown." You look in another dictionary and it says "gray" or "blue" or even something called "moleskin." It's a chameleon color.

So all you have to do is show a swatch of taupe to your trustees. Each one will think that it is her color, and your problems will be solved.

Peace,
Will

Chain Saw Violence Is Perfectly Normal from Library Directors Who Have Just Opened New Buildings

Dear Will,

By nature I am not a psychotic person. If, for instance, I were to invite you over to my house for dinner, I wouldn't demand that you take your shoes off. You can walk on my carpet with combat boots if you so desire just as long as you wipe your feet on the welcome mat

first. And if you did decide to take your shoes off and get comfortable, by all means, it would be fine with me if you wanted to prop your feet up on the coffee table while reading the newspaper or watching television.

Ordinarily I like to think of myself as an informal, "life is too short to worry about footprints in the carpeting" kind of woman. Walk into my office and you'll see creative clutter on my desk and a wall full of woeful watercolors painted by my first grade daughter. Spit and polish I am not and never have been. There will always be a run in my stockings and a hole in my sweater, but, hey, I'm happy,

which is a lot more than you can say about the new professional
woman who has an anxiety attack every time someone gets a felt-
tipped pen anywhere near the sleeve of her Liz Claiborne dress. On
my desk is a little sign that says "Pobody's Nerfect!"

When talking about happiness, however, I should actually be using the past tense because three short weeks ago during an intense
period of self-examination in front of my bedroom mirror I detected
a rather startling change in my usually happy-go-lucky face. Instead
of a smile I saw a frown. It was a frown of jealousy.

A little bit of background information will explain if not cure my
recent attitudinal metamorphosis from "what me worry" to "where's
my freaking chain saw." The last six years of my life have been
almost entirely devoted to financing, designing, and constructing a
new 57,000 square foot main building for the regional library district
that I direct. Three weeks ago on a serene Sunday afternoon the
library had its grand opening with all the normal pomp and cir-
cumstance. Happily there was a noticeable lack of criticism about the
new building. Everyone apparently considers it a successful project
in that the library is not egregiously ugly, noticeably dysfunctional,
or ostentatiously expensive. These are, I have decided, the three big
tests for any building constructed with taxpayers' money.

Relieved as I am by the taxpayers' acceptance of the building, I
am not all that fond of them walking on the new carpeting without
taking their shoes off. Our library district is located in a primarily
agricultural area which means that our new carpeting is unfortunately being exposed to a diverse array of manures.

But my frustrations go far beyond the new carpeting. The truth
is I simply can't bear the thought of the great unwashed public having anything to do with my library at all. My life, six years of it
anyway, are in that building. If I really wanted to be melodramatic I
could say that the building cost me my marriage. Jonathan warned
me – "If you bring those drawings home one more time, I'm moving
out" – and true to his word, he moved out. To be honest, that was not
a tragedy. Jonathan hadn't held a job for years and the great
American novel he was writing was up to 1200 manuscript pages and
not even halfway completed. Good riddance.

As disconnected as I had become to Jonathan that's how attached
I became to my library. I loved everything about the building – the
way the circulation desk jutted out toward the front entry in a bold

45 degree angle, the way the granite of the inner lobby just sort of evolved into the carpeting of the reading areas, the way the arched back of the study chairs combined both classical and minimalist elements, and the way sunlight filtered through the oblong window in the children's room to the story hour amphitheater below.

Until the grand opening, this place had been mine. Now it belonged to the public – a public that would track up its carpeting, chip the paint off its walls, and rub the varnish off its woodwork. I became jealous. The building, like an obscure actor who had suddenly scored a major cinematic hit, now beonged to everyone. So deep goes my jealousy rage that I now find myself contemplating chain saw terror toward the people I see propping their feet on the octagonal study desks. Don't they know how hard I worked designing those desks?

Since they say that you can measure the depth of a person's psychosis by the degree of hostility that it produces, I guess I am in great need of intensive psychiatric care? Am I right?

Sincerely,
PROBABLY CERTIFIABLE

Dear Probably,

Ordinarily I would say that intense chain saw fantasies are not symptomatic of a real healthy person, but in your case I'm not worried. Your situation is perfectly normal – there is even a clinical acronym for it: PLBS (Post Library Building Syndrome). It manifests itself through intermittent periods of depression and hostility. If untreated, PLBS can be serious. There are known cases where library directors suffering from PLBS have acted out their fantasies so I wouldn't be checking out the want-ads for good buys on chain saws if I were you.

My strong suggestion is that YOU GET OUT OF TOWN FOR AT LEAST SIX WEEKS AND NOT, GOD FORBID, TO ANY LIBRARY CONFERENCES. Like most library directors suffering from PBLS you probably have at least that much vacation saved up since you obviously didn't take any time off during the duration of your project (which is of course why you are so nuts now).

Search the map for a warm beach. Go there. And stay there.

Spend your days drinking something alcoholic out of a pineapple and your nights drinking something alcoholic out of a coconut. Count grains of sand and look at the clouds.

In six weeks you'll be cured. Then you might want to sign up for A.A.

Regards,
Dr. Will

Husbands Always Look Better
When They Are Dead

Dear Will,

The world has changed in so many ways since I started working here at the library that's it hard to know exactly where to start.

I suppose the first thing I should tell you is that I've announced that I'll be retiring next year on February 16th, which is the very day I started my career here, 41 years ago. I was 24 at the time and fresh out of library school. The year was 1952. It was the beginning of the Eisenhower era. I was a cataloger. In those days we didn't have networks or computers or even cataloging in publication data. You did your own cataloging.

Original cataloging was, I liked to think, a kind of art form. At least I thought of myself as an artist. I took delight in the idiosyncrasies of our library's catalog. Can you believe that in 1952 we were still doing some of our cards in long hand? Although the shortage of typewriters from the war years had long since ended, we had a clerk on staff who had taken some calligraphy courses from a private teacher.

Her script was so beautiful that we allowed her to stay on even though she refused to learn how to type. She did all the cards for our fiction books in her elegant script. If I remember correctly she used an elegant antique fountain pen – a Parker Brothers I think it was – that she filled with indelible black ink. To protect her clothes she wore an artist's smock.

Since all of the cards for our nonfiction books were typewritten on a squatty old Royal 100, we ended up with a most unusual catalog—one that was truly distinctive. I daresay that even today it might be called "user friendly" in that our patrons could immediately tell, just from the appearance of the catalog card, if a title were fiction or nonfiction.

But time unfortunately marches unstoppably along, and our handsome old card catalog became as outdated as my once sporty Studebaker Lark. I'm a sentimental old fool, and I managed to salvage a small section of the catalog from the dumpster truck. I'm glad I did because it looks just fine against the brick wall of my kitchen, and it comes in handy too. I've put my recipes into its drawers, and I've perched my microwave oven on its top shelf right where we used to keep a big heavy book of subject headings for patrons to consult, which of course they never did.

I stayed in cataloging for five years and then was transferred to reference. Mr. Fitzhugh, my director—bless him—told me that I was "just too lovely to be hidden away in a stuffy old cataloging room." And then he added, after he could see that I wasn't doing any cartwheels, "You'll never catch a man back there!"

I hemmed and hawed and reminded him that I had hired on as a cataloger and that's exactly what I always wanted to be, but secretly I was pleased. It was, to be honest with you, getting a bit dusty back there with Sears and Dewey, and I really couldn't picture myself as a cataloger for life. The cataloging room just had too much of the fragrance of dried flowers and floor wax. I wanted out, and Mr. Fitzhugh, to my surprise, sensed that.

I spent five years at reference, and Mr. Fitzhugh was right—I met a man, a young and handsome family doctor in town who wanted to know what a share of Studebaker stock was selling for on December 31, 1957 (I'll never forget that date). He was doing his income tax and was in a frightful hurry.

I couldn't help him right away since I was handling a phone call, so I waved him back to the corner of the reference room where the old *Wall Street Journals* were stacked one on top of the other on some rickety old steel shelving that Frank our janitor had been promising to fix for a month of Sundays. Do you know that in his haste to get the issue he desired, that doctor knocked over the entire shelving unit? I remember thinking at the time that the young fool was lucky he hadn't killed himself. That's how Ned and I met. Three years later we were married, and we stayed married (as happy as a pair of clams) until Ned passed away four years ago. Cancer.

In 1963, Miss Tulley, Mr. Fitzhugh's assistant, retired to a cute little tile and stucco bungalow in Clearwater, Florida, and I was promoted. At the time, Mr. Fitzhugh told me that in four years he would be retiring and that he planned to train me so that I could take over for him when the time came.

Things went pretty much according to plan, and despite some resistance from Dr. Maxwell, who was president of the Library Board and who just never did warm up to the idea of a woman in management, I became director in 1967. With all modesty aside, I can say that the 25 years of my directorship were fruitful ones. We built a much needed branch on the north end of town (it was named in honor of Mr. Fitzhugh), we computerized our circulation and cataloging operations, and we even managed to bring our book budget up to A.L.A. standards.

Now here's my problem: I have decided I don't want to leave! I know that I have been here for over 40 years and that I'm 65 years old and that I've already announced my retirement and that the board is already forming a search committee and that it's only fair that I step aside and give a young person the same opportunity that Miss Tulley and Mr. Fitzhugh gave me, but recently I've been thinking and wondering about my life away from this place and it scares me. There's no other way to say it—I'm scared.

If Ned were still alive it would be different. But I'm alone now and probably always will be. We never had any children, and I know that I'll never find anyone who is half the man that Ned was.

I want to stay active. The thought of moving off to some trailer park in Florida or Arizona simply fills me with the horror of being buried alive. The truth is I am as good a library director today as I was twenty years ago—probably better. I'm physically healthy, mentally sharp, and I can beat any of those young whippersnappers at the reference desk in an on-line search. I am not a relic!

Yes, I want desperately to call off the retirement and stay here, right here in my library. I'm neither ready to die nor retire! Do I dare inform the board that rumors of my demise are quite premature?

Sincerely,
SARAH

Dear Sarah,

I'm quite taken with your fondness for the past and your enthusiasm for the future. By all means call off the retirement party! And don't call for another one until you have to be carried off! We need people like you in the profession for protection against "the young whippersnappers." Heck if Reagan could run the country at 80, you're certainly able to run your library at 65. I should think your board, with the exception of that horrid Dr. Maxwell (hopefully *he's* dead), would welcome your change of heart. I'm sure they were not at all looking forward to replacing you.

Now after telling you how great you are, I must tell you something that you don't want to hear. It's time to stop mourning Ned. He couldn't have been that wonderful. Husbands always look better dead than alive. Certainly he left his socks lying around, and surely he never made a bed in his life. The point is, Sarah, your personal life did not have to die when Ned died. To paraphrase a favorite person of yours, you're just too lovely to stay hidden behind a veil of mourning.

You've got to let his memory go. Get a little crazy, Sarah. Go dancing! Take a cruise! Getting thrust back into the singles jungle can certainly be a shock, but hey it's been four years since Ned died.

So... Don't quit your job, Sarah, but don't quit your life either.

Best Regards,
Will

*   *   *

People Go to Work Forty Hours a Week to Get Away from Their Spouse

Dear Will,

How do you feel about married people working together in the same library? Recently two of my reference librarians (we have a six

person reference department) tied the knot, and my life as their supervisor has TURNED INTO KNOTS.

The husband is one of those people who enjoys wearing a "Question Authority" button. Although extremely competent, he carries an organizational chip on his shoulder. In his mind he is the oppressed worker and I am the exploitive manager. He's very much into an "us" against "them" working relationship.

Up until the wedding, his wife and I had enjoyed a warm and cooperative working relationship. Now things have changed. Although she is not yet wearing a "Question Authority" button, she is developing an attitude similar to his. For instance, she will not do the little things that she used to do like shelving a stray reference book or putting scratch pads out at the index tables because these things are "not in the job description."

I went out to lunch with her to talk about her attitude problem and she sincerely promised to try to be more cooperative. But the next day (after she had obviously had a long talk with her husband), she was back to being peevish and intransigent.

Any suggestions?

> Sincerely,
> TIED UP IN KNOTS

Dear Knots,

Do nothing. I guarantee that this problem will work itself out. As much as I love my wife there is no way that I could ever imagine working with her at my place of employment. I'm sure she feels the same way about me.

I am thoroughly convinced that one of the main reasons people go to work 40 hours a week is to get away from their spouse. Marriage is a fragile, delicate thing. It is not enhanced when the husband and wife see too much of each other.

In time (four to six months) one of five things will happen: (1) the wife will kill the husband, (2) the husband will kill the wife, (3) there will be a divorce, (4) the husband will find another job, or (5) the wife will find another job. Just have patience.

> Regards,
> Will

The Only Heat Coming from Your Boiler Room Should Be in Pipes

Dear Will,

Our janitor, Ben, is like the dog who chases after the milk truck. If he ever did catch up with the truck he wouldn't know what to do.

All you have to do is spend ten minutes with Ben and I guarantee he'd be trying to convince you that he had made love to more women that Hugh Hefner. Ben, of course, is all talk. If he ever did, God forbid, get a woman into a compromising position he would have absolutely no idea of how to proceed. He's like a lot of guys I knew in high school – all talk and no action.

But a big thing with Ben is maintaining appearances. To further his image as a womanizer he has decorated his boiler room in a sort of postmodern, blue collar pornographic chic. It's pretty heady stuff, so heady that a number of white collar males on our staff seem to have developed an unusually active interest in the operation and maintenance of the library's boiler system.

For four and a half years his tastes in interior decoration offended no one. But then Mozelle came to work and Ben's pinups became an issue. Mozelle, the library's cleaning lady, hangs her coat and hat up in the boiler room when she comes to work every morning, and to say the last, she is not amused by Ben's tastes in photography.

For the first three months that she worked here, she and Ben waged an on-going battle that all of us on staff watched with a sort of bemused curiosity. Each morning Mozelle, after hanging up her hat and coat, would take the pin-ups down, and each evening, after she had gone home, Ben would hang them back up.

Now the war has escalated. Mozelle has come to me (I'm the director) and in no uncertain terms has served notice that if I do not forbid the pinups that she will bring a sexual harassment complaint against Ben and me.

Personally, I don't care about the pinups. It's not like I go down to the boiler room everyday to look at them. But I'm afraid that if I tell Ben to take them down, he will get mad and quit, which is the last thing I want to have happen because as janitors go Ben is not bad. He is not a thief or a drunk, and he does know how this old building of ours works. It would be hard to replace him.

The way I see it, Ben is entitled to his idiosyncrasies. It's not like he's touching or pinching anyone.

What do you think I should do?

Sincerely,
BILL

Dear Bill,

Get the pinups down – NOW. Federal courts have heard several sexual harassment cases that deal specifically with nude pictures on office walls. In each case the court decided that the display of pinups does in fact constitute sexual harassment.

Case closed. Clean up your act, Bill.

Regards,
Will

Even the Rev. Bakker Used a Motel Room

Dear Will,

I am the director of a public library in a community of 10,000 in the Bible Belt of the Deep South. Our town is friendly. Everyone knows the mayor by his first name, and the weekly newspaper tells who you had over for dinner last week. To get a picture of what our community is like just think of Andy Griffith's Mayberry.

Last Sunday morning about a half-hour before church I stopped by my office to pick up my umbrella. It looked like rain. The library was closed and I entered through the back door.

What do you suppose I saw in the reference room? Eva Leigh Jenkins was in an advanced state of physical affection with the Reverend Douglas Dacker. Eva Leigh is my reference librarian, and

the Reverend Dacker is the pastor of the Church of God, which is the church of choice for 80 percent of our Godfearing citizens.

I am quite certain that neither Eva Leigh or the Reverend saw me. They were pretty much wrapped up in each other. I don't know what to do or say. The Rev. Dacker is married to Janie May Dacker, my children's librarian, and Eva Leigh is dating Dr. Sparks, who just so happens to be vice chair of my board of trustees.

The domino effect potential for the library in this situation is almost staggering to imagine. Also, the grapevine in our town is so widespread that if I were to mention what I saw to anyone it would be all over town by tomorrow at dinner time.

I don't want to ruin anybody's life but what Eva Leigh and the Rev. Dacker did was not only wrong, it was stupid as well! Actually I am not surprised by Dacker's behavior since he has come on to me on several occasions (all attempts were thwarted to be sure) but I am shocked by Eva Leigh.

What should I do?
BETWEEN A ROCK AND A HARD PLACE

Dear Rock,

If this had taken place anywhere but in the library, I would advise you to do absolutely nothing.

Since, however, your reference room was most assuredly being used for activities not intended by the town fathers, you cannot simply look the other way. Even the reverends Bakker and Swaggart had the decency to conduct their private activities in the privacy of a motel room. Eva Leigh and Douglas should have done the same.

Very discreetly pull Eva Leigh aside, tell her what you saw, and advise her to conduct her soap opera in a setting that will not bring scandal upon the library. Tell her of the domino effect, and leave it at that.

Do no more; do no less.

Regards,
Will

Good Times Are Not Had on Bathroom Walls

Dear Will,

Moral dilemmas are never like what they described in my catechism class in the third grade. I've tried, I really have, to follow the teachings of the good sisters who taught me about right and wrong in the third grade, but I'm not perfect. Is any man?

Here's my dilemma: Yesterday while on duty at the reference

desk I was forced to use the public men's room. The staff bathroom is clear up on the third floor and I didn't have much time since I was the only one staffing the desk. On the wall above the urinals there was written in a rather attractive mock English gothic script the following message: "FOR A GOOD TIME CALL 131-9996."

It just so happens that at that point in my life the idea of a good time had a great deal of appeal for me. I don't want to make any excuses but consider how bad things had gotten for me: (1) two months earlier my wife left me not for another man but for a woman, (2) a week ago I backed right into my garage door, destroying it and totaling my Honda Civic, (3) three days ago I was diagnosed as having incipient gum disease, and (4) last night my 19-year-old son called from college and said that one of his professors had created a complex mathematical model of the universe on his laptop computer that provided irrefutable evidence that God does not exist.

That's why I was ready for a good time. So as soon as I saw the inviting gothic script on the wall in front of me I instinctively reached for my pen and wrote the phone number down on my wrist.

That night on my way home I stopped at Syncopation for happy hour. There was no way that I was going to call for a good time without the benefit of three banana daiquiris which I promptly drank. Then from the toll phone in the back of the bar I dialed what I hoped would be my lucky number. An answering machine clicked on—"Leave your data after the beep and I'll get back to you toute suite."

As soon as I heard the words "toute suite" I hung up and asked the barkeep to hurry out a fourth daiquiri. The message left me stunned. There is only one person in the whole world who would use the phrase "toute suite" on an answering machine message—Chelli Fairfield, one of our children's librarians. The use of the word "data" also suggested a librarian.

It wasn't all that much of a shock actually because Chelli has a reputation for being very creative in a promiscuous sense. But had she devolved to the point of advertising her services on the bathroom walls of her place of employment? That didn't make sense but who else could it be? Her voice, just like the voice on the machine, is a rather unmistakable mix of Meryl Streep and Mae West.

I instinctively checked the phone book. Chelli was not listed. Apparently she prefers to have her number listed on bathroom walls. I

went back to the bar and had a fifth daiquiri
and then a sixth and told the bartender
that I would give him five dollars if
he called 131-9996 and negotiated a
good time.

For ten dollars he called. In his
words: "The lady was very nice, her
rates were not out of line with current
market conditions, her trysting place was
fairly standard – the Red Antler Motel and
Motor Lodge, and what does toute suite
mean."

So what should I do – have a seventh
daiquiri and forget the whole thing, call
the police, or report her to Miss Wiggins,
our director?

Sincerely,
RALPH

Dear Ralph,

Have the seventh daiquiri and forget the whole thing unless you
want to put yourself in the embarrassing position of explaining to
Miss Wiggins why you were calling a number that you got off a bathroom wall. It sounds like you have enough problems of your own.
Just remember Chelli wouldn't be in business without guys like you.

Regards,
Will

For Necktie Abuse
Get Out the Scissors

Dear Will,

They say it's the little things that drive people crazy and I agree.
Remember that movie where the wife shoots the husband because

after thirty years of being married to him she suddenly decides that she can no longer tolerate the disgusting way he chews his meat? To me that's scary.

Who's to say that something equally annoying couldn't generate a similarly violent impulse in any one of us? I'm absolutely convinced that given the right set of circumstances the gentlest person alive is capable of committing the most unspeakable violence with a simple butter knife.

I raise this issue because the limits of my civility are being tested by my co-worker on the reference desk. He continually tucks his necktie into his pants. Have you ever heard of anything so goofy?

The first time I saw this I thought that he had gotten dressed in a hurry and had simply miscalculated the length of his tie. But now that he has done it 379 working days in a row I am convinced that in his own demented mind he thinks he is making some kind of a fashion statement. I cringe everytime I see him, which is like four thousand times a day.

Don't worry, I have raised this issue with Janet, our supervisor. But she is of no help. She thinks my objections are silly bordering on fussy. "He's a male librarian," she says, "and by definition all male librarians are geeks. Just be thankful he doesn't come to work in sneakers or, worse yet, white shoes."

Needless to say I think Janet's attitude toward male librarians is regrettably cavalier. She should not stereotype with such a broad brush. I know a few male librarians who are almost normal, and my co-worker is not a congenitally geekish person. Sure, he is quiet and overly sensitive, but he does have a decent skin complexion and he's only got one small bald spot on the back of his head. If he would wear his ties properly he would look halfway normal.

Myself, I take a great deal of pride in the way I look (this past year I spent over $4000 on my wardrobe) and I really don't appreciate working with someone who tucks his tie into his pants. It makes me look bad by association. I'm totally embarrassed and on edge.

Would it be inappropriate for me to give him some friendly fashion advice?

Sincerely,
PRISCELLA

Dear Priscella,

By all means give him your views. That's certainly preferable to assaulting him with a butter knife. I agree with you completely about everything. Tucking a tie into your pants is so egregiously inane that it should be punishable by law.

Yes, please tell this man that he looks idiotic, and if he persists in tucking his tie into his pants, simply take some scissors and cut his tie just above the belt level (which is where most neckware experts suggest that a tie should hang). Keep cutting his ties until he gets the message.

We librarians all suffer when one of our colleagues looks like a geek.

Sincerely,
Will

He Who Lives By the Stereotype
Will Die By the Stereotype

Dear Will,

Think of the lowliest professionals on the face of the earth. I'm talking about the lowest of the low. Why they require a college degree for this work I have no idea. I mean this is the most unprofessional profession there is.

I am, of course, talking about the parks and recreation profession. Well, I know that the country needs an occupation for all its washed up jocks to be gainfully employed, but really do they have to call it a profession? Those of us in legitimate professions have every right in the world to be upset that the Neanderthals who do parks and recreation work are called professionals. It's like calling Andrew Dice Clay a social commentator.

Ordinarily I don't sit around thinking of insulting things to say about ex-jocks, but today I'm motivated because I have just learned that our public library will be merged with our city's parks and recreation unit into something that will bureaucratically be called a Leisure Services Department.

This is the most degrading thing that has ever happened to me as a library director. To lump the library with a glorified municipal P.E. program is like mating the Pope with Madonna. I'm not saying that softball and volleyball leagues are inherently bad, but they certainly bear no relation to the library. We're not even distant cousins with those people. We librarians provide important informational and educational services – they provide frivolous playtime activities.

Sincerely,
MADDER THAN THE DICKENS

Dear Dickens,

Cool off. Isn't it wonderfully ironic that someone in the library profession such as yourself would so unmercifully attack another professional group with such a scathing stereotype. Of course we librarians have never suffered from any unfair image problems, have we?

Isn't it equally ironic that a librarian would so vehemently attack the whole notion of recreation and leisure services? Where have you been during the last fifteen years? Don't you know that the whole public library profession over that time period has been enthralled with a "give 'em what they want" service orientation?

I'm glad you think that a public library is essentially an informational and educational service because a lot of your fellow professionals (who are providing the public with millions of dollars worth of frivolous beach books, video games, and blockbuster movies) don't. As a result of their mischief, we are now obviously and unfortunately being seen as recreation professionals ourselves. Your merger is a good case in point.

Having said that, let me also say that such a merger has tremendous advantages. When we are organizationally linked with the recreation department our own purpose becomes more sharply focused, and we can begin to see the futility of trying to be something (a recreation service) that we should not. We begin to see the waste involved in duplicating municipal services. Let the recreation profession take care of recreation, and let the library profession take care of information and education.

We have distinctly different jobs to do, and we both do them well. Yes, that's right. The average recreation professional is no more a Neanderthal than the average librarian is a wimp.

Regards,
Will

*   *   *

It's Better to Be Truthful Than Dead

Dear Will,

Pot lucks are cherished social events in our library. We have 20 employees on staff, which is about the perfect number for a pot luck. With 20 people bringing in food you get just the right diversity of dishes without being overwhelmed. My observation is that the pleasures of a pot luck are two-fold: you get to enjoy a wide variety of food, and you get to see a wide variety of people enjoying the food that you prepared. This is to say nothing of the warm feelings of camaraderie that are created when co-workers get together in a friendly environment to enjoy each other's company and conversation.

Traditionally we have four potlucks each year oriented around the major holidays—Christmas/Channukah, Easter/Passover, the Fourth of July, and Thanksgiving. We all much prefer the lunchtime potluck approach to having a group dinner at a restaurant or an evening party at somebody's house, and for the first nine years that I worked at the library (in the circulation department) I would have to say that each pot luck was a big success.

But ever since Alvin came to work in reference two years ago everything has changed. First of all, Alvin is a very nice person. He's the person on staff who you leave your cat with when you go on vacation. He's the person who will drive you to the service station so that you can pick up your car after it's been fixed. He's the person who will lend you $20 when you come up short at the end of the week. He's just a very nice person who wants everyone to like him.

Unfortunately Alvin is a very horrible cook, only he doesn't know that. He thinks he's a gourmet chef, and all the externals would point to such a conclusion. Just visit the kitchen. He has a veritable fortune invested in pots, pans, knives, woks, food processors, cookbooks, and every other culinary accessory imaginable. None of that helps. Alvin's food creations taste like monkey excrement.

We were introduced to his cooking soon after we met him. As a goodwill gesture, he left a plate of what appeared to be rather normal brownies in the staff lounge on the day he started work here.

Word quickly spread from Sylvia, our resident chocolate expert, that you wouldn't want to feed Alvin's brownies to your dog, and to prevent group food poisoning she promptly dumped them into the garbage disposal. Alvin, of course, assumed that they disappeared so rapidly because they were so irresistibly delicious.

Then came the Thanksgiving pot luck. With great fanfare Alvin brought a three bean casserole that he said was a special family recipe. "Make sure that you try my casserole first," he said with obvious pride and delight. To be polite I tried it under his watchful eyes and consider myself noble for not vomiting right there on the spot. Fortunately I was able to get to the bathroom. It was monkey excrement, pure monkey excrement. But since Alvin is such a nice person everybody forced themselves to eat at least a spoonful of his concoction. Obviously a lot of people spent that pot luck in the bathroom.

Succeeding pot lucks have followed that pattern. Alvin shows up with a smile and a dish and everybody gets sick. He just gets really offended if you don't try his food, and he is such a nice person that it breaks your heart to see him get hurt. Nobody has the heart to tell him that he is giving people indigestion. Rather than confront him with the truth, we are now talking about discontinuing the pot lucks and going out to a restaurant at night for dinner. But nobody really likes that option. If only Alvin would just bring a bag of potato chips like the other two men on the staff do everything would be just fine.

What should we do?

Sincerely,

AMANDA

Dear Amanda,

Tell Alvin the truth before somebody dies of poisoning. Since he is so sensitive do it diplomatically but firmly. For instance you might say, "Alvin, we like you. You're a wonderful reference librarian and an admirable human being. But your cooking tastes like monkey excrement. At the next pot luck please bring potato chips and don't open the bag until you get here."

This approach should work. If you are not willing to deal with the problem head on, however, you might assign somebody to bring a gallon size bottle of Pepto Bismol to your next pot luck.

Regards,

Will

Beware of Holistic Working Environments

Dear Will,

I don't consider myself to be old, inflexible, or behind the times, but I am very disturbed about what is happening in the library where I work.

First of all, I am a circulation clerk. Granted, I don't have an M.L.S. or even a B.A. which, heaven knows, around here you would think is a personal disgrace. Why are professional librarians so degree conscious? Why do they feel they need to cloak themselves with their academic credentials? Is it because they make so little money?

The point is I simply don't understand what is going on around here anymore. Three months ago we got a new director from California who promised everybody that he intended to create a holistic working environment – one that would be humane and sensitive to the needs of the library employees. He claims that organizations today must deal with their employees as complete persons – not just as 8 to 5 drones.

True to his word he called each and every one of us into a private two hour meeting. The purpose of the meeting was for what he called "mutual enlightenment." "I want to get to know you and I want you to get to know me. Bottom line is I want you to see me as a caring and sharing person and not as a boss." Well I have to tell you that he told me a lot more about himself than I ever wanted to know.

It wasn't so bad when he was talking about his hobbies (bird watching and organic gardening) but when he got into his sob story about being beaten by an abusive father I began to feel very uncomfortable. This discomfort quickly turned into embarrassment when he began to talk about his marital history (stormy) and his sexual preferences (eclectic).

I became so uncomfortable that I told him that I wanted to end the meeting and return to the circ desk. In response, he suggested that I was too uptight and that I should get rolfed. I told him that I was horrified that he would suggest such a thing. But he remained calm. "Don't overreact," he said. "Although initially rolfing can be painful, it is an effective holistic therapy. I plan on making it the foundation of our staff wellness program."

Will, please tell me – is rolfing what I think it is?

Sincerely,
ALL I WANT IS TO BE LEFT
ALONE TO WORK CIRCULATION

Dear Alone,

No, rolfing is not what you think it is. It is a quasi chiropractic technique that attempts to rearrange the muscles in your back, which is not exactly what I would call a mainstream medical therapy.

Your director should in no way be involved in prescribing rolfing or any other type of physical therapy for you. Furthermore his little fireside chat with you violated several sexual harassment laws.

My advice is for you to call an attorney and get this quack locked up.

Regards,
Will

The Home Office Concept Will Do Wonders for Soap Opera Ratings

Dear Will,

One of my acquisitions librarians is seven months pregnant. Yesterday she presented me with a well thought out and very detailed proposal to work at home during the remaining two months of her pregnancy and for the first three years of her child's life. "Just until my child is ready to go to preschool," is the way she put it.

Her justification for this arrangement is two-fold. First, she says with a telephone, a computer terminal, a phone modem, and a fax machine she can be just as accessible and productive at home as she currently is at the library. Second she feels that this set-up is only fair since our college is not enlightened enough to have a day care program for employees' children.

I keep reading that the home office is the wave of the future, so my inclination is to allow her to do this.

What do you think?

Sincerely,
PEGGY

Dear Peggy,

My very strong opinion is that the home office is splendid for someone who works independently and is self-employed. But as an alternative arrangement for employees who are part of an organization like a library I think it stinks.

If you allow this acquisitions librarian to work at home, you'd better be prepared to do the same for others on your staff who make a similar request. It's not fair (or legal) to offer a benefit to one employee without offering it to others who do comparable work. Certainly if I were a cataloger or acquisitions librarian in your library I would want to work at home. Who wouldn't? You'd save on gas, clothes, day-care, and the television is only a step away.

Regards,
Will

Festschriften Should Always Be Served at Room Temperature

Dear Will,

Here's a thumbnail sketch of my life:

(a) I was a straight A student in high school and got a 1486 on my S.A.T.
(b) I got a B.A. degree from Radcliffe (English literature) and a husband from Harvard (securities analyst).
(c) I reproduced every three years for the first nine years of my marriage (two boys, one girl).
(d) I divorced my husband two months after our twentieth anniversary for adultery, mental cruelty, and dislike of my Indian pottery collection.
(e) I am now 45 years old and my children are 21, 18, and 15.

After I divorced my husband (four years ago) I had to find a job. Does it say something about our society that my Radcliffe degree qualified me to pour coffee, deep-fry chicken nuggets, go to real estate school, sell Avon, and work in the local library? I chose to work in the local public library.

I am what is called a library assistant in the reference department. If libraries were golf courses I would be called a caddy because what I do is all the little things that the librarians feel is beneath their professional dignity. I file pocket parts, shelve books, check in microfiche, process telephone books, compile booklists – that sort of thing.

Sometimes, when one of the librarians is sick or when things get particularly crazy, I am even allowed to provide reference service – up to a point. They let me show patrons how to use the on-line catalog but they don't actually let me answer reference questions (like I don't know how to look up the value of the yen in the *Wall Street Journal*).

I've been a library assistant now for four years, and don't get me wrong, I absolutely love the job – being around books and people is right where I want to be. But as much as I like it, I'm getting frustrated – exasperated is more like it. Even without a master's degree in library science, I know that I can do as good a job as any of the professional reference librarians on our staff, and in some cases I can do much better.

Take Darrel, our science and technology specialist. He's what I would call a dysfunctional human being – the quintessential library dweeb. The rumor is that he has a near genius level I.Q. but really how would you know? Not only does he not talk, he purposefully avoids people. He likes to withdraw into his own little world. It's too bad he wasn't born a mollusk. One of the librarians on the night shift told me that Darrel's been in therapy for years. The jury is out about whether he actually hates people or is simply scared of them. It's to the point now that all Darrel does is stay in the backroom and write annotated bibliographies. Our reference supervisor, Sydney, keeps him on because he says our library has the best annotated bibliographies in the country.

And then there's Fay. Fay is also dysfunctional, which I'm told by a counseler friend of mine is the current euphemism for psychotic. Her personality disorder is way beyond arrogance. She's into some heavy hostility toward the human race. She starts out every reference interview by interrupting the patron and asking the question, "Why do you want to know?". She does this because it's a matter of principle with her not to help with homework assignments, not to settle bets, not to assist bill collectors, and not to aid medical patients with self diagnosis. Sydney keeps her on because she happens to be the only person in the department who can fix the microfilm machine when it's broken.

I watch this professional weirdness every day and think how unfair it is for me – a Radcliffe graduate – not to be eligible for a promotion to professional status simply because I don't have the sacred M.L.S. from an A.L.A. approved library school.

I've done some checking and discovered that the closest A.L.A. approved library school is 500 miles away in a neighboring state. The local university has a school of education, law, medicine, and theology but not librarianship, which means it's easier for me to become a doctor, lawyer, teacher, or minister than a librarian. Doesn't this strike you as a little strange?

I happen to have a theory. My theory is that the library profession is made up of very dysfunctional people like Darrel and Fay and Sydney who want to make it very, very difficult for talented, intelligent, and normal people like myself to get certified. You know how some cities build shelters for homeless people? Well, I think that A.L.A. has built an occupational shelter for dysfunctional people with M.L.S. degrees by accrediting only 50-some library schools. Do you realize that there is not one accredited library school in the entire state of Minnesota but there are two in the city of Denton, Texas? Personally, I wouldn't go to Denton, Texas, even if it was the last place on earth to buy ice cream.

Yesterday I asked Sydney why I needed an M.L.S. to do reference work. He looked down at me like I had some disgusting skin disease and said in a very haughty voice, "Festschriften." Then he walked away.

Will, what gives?

Sincerely,
A FUNCTIONAL PERSON TRYING TO GET
INTO A DYSFUNCTIONAL PROFESSION

Dear Functional,

I'd say you have some dysfunctionalities of your own. First, no one gives a hoot that you went to Radcliffe. I'm sure you're very bright, but really when you get to be 45 years old the last thing people want to know about you is where you went to college. Second, you cannot lay judgment on an entire profession based on three weird people. If you want to talk weird just start poking around the legal and medical professions. That's where you'll find weird. The fact is most of the professional librarians I have met are very nice, normal, helpful, and intelligent people. We may not have a lot of flash and dazzle but we are very nice. The planet would be a much better place if it were populated entirely by librarians. If librarians ran things there might be a lot more committees in the world, but there wouldn't be any wars, and all things considered I'd rather have committees than wars.

Having said this, I agree with the gist of your letter. You are entirely correct. The paucity of library schools makes it far too difficult for people like yourself to become accredited librarians. My solution is simple: the M.L.S. degree should be obtainable through all graduate schools of education. This system works well for the school library profession. Why not extend it to public, academic, and special libraries as well?

Finally, Sydney's rather cryptic remark about Festschriften is very telling. Every profession has its own language. Sit down with a bunch of lawyers and you'll find yourself in a foreign country. They have a language of their own. The same holds true for engineers, accountants, doctors, and every other professional group. What Sydney is suggesting is that you don't know the language of librarianship, therefore you can't be a member of the club. Professional librarians love to use fancy words and "Festschriften" is one of the fanciest.

I will be honest, until I looked the word up in the A.L.A. Glossary, I thought it referred to a fish salad that is supposed to be served at room temperature. I was only half right. Festschriften are special commemerative publications in honor of someone or something. They are, however, served at room temperature.

Finally, don't put down Denton, Texas. I've been there, and I think it is a lovely place.

Regards,
Will

*   *   *

The Boss Is Always Wrong

Dear Will,

Recently a team of consultants did a thorough investigation of all our city departments to assess something called "organization climate." To my chagrin their study revealed that the climate in the library (I am the director), while not stormy, is definitely on the damp and drizzly side.

This came as quite a shock to me. I had thought that everything was rather hunky-dory, but according to the consultants there are a lot of unhappy library employees. Apparently the greatest unhappiness has to do with organizational communication and decision-making.

To be honest, I have no idea where or how to begin the process of creating a positive work environment and rebuilding staff morale. What is your advice?

Sincerely,
BEWILDERED

Dear Bewildered,

Don't be upset about what the consultants said about your organization. There isn't a library in the world that is perfect.

You could start your rebuilding program by reading any one of the twenty thousand books that have been written on this subject since the Japanese started destroying us in world markets. But most of those books offer little more than glittering generalities like "empower your employees." So don't waste your time. I, on the other hand, can tell you everything you need to know in three short paragraphs, so read carefully.

The truth is your library is not one single organization. It is actually a lot of little organizations. Each work unit (cataloging, reference, children's, circulation, etc.) is actually a separate organization. With that fact in mind go back to your consultants' study and read it in more detail. I think that you will find that the climate in some work units is sunnier than in others. What makes the difference? Why, for instance, is the cataloging department happier than

the reference department? The answer is simple. The most important factor in determining employee morale is the quality of the supervisor/employee relationship that exists in each of your work units.

There are two types of supervisors – facilitators and bosses. Work units with facilitator supervisors will always have an excellent working climate. Work units with boss supervisors will always have a poor working climate. Bosses dictate; facilitators communicate. Bosses rule by fear and intimidation; facilitators motivate through praise and encouragement. The boss is top dog; the facilitator is first among equals. To create a good working environment in your library all you have to do is teach your bosses to become facilitators.

Organizational climate depends less on who is at the top of an organizational chart and more on who is in the middle of it. Mother Theresa could be the library director but if she had ineffective bosses in her supervisory positions it wouldn't make any difference. She too would have poor employee morale. Having a bad boss is like being married to the wrong person.

Regards,
Will

When You Get Remarried
Don't Talk About Your Ex-husband
Like He Is God

Dear Will,

Five months ago the woman who directed our library for the past 33 years retired, and we got a new director who brought with her a new organization chart, a new employee evaluation process, a new set of job titles and job descriptions, a new book selection policy, a new patron complaint policy, and a new circulation policy. It's really very hard to think of anything that she hasn't changed.

These changes are certainly unsettling but after 33 years of the same library director, we were braced for change. It is our new director's attitude that we object to. She thinks that the library gospel was written at her previous library, Auburn Public, where she was the assistant director.

I'm serious, if she says, "Back at Auburn Public we did it this way," one more time she very well could find herself assassinated. She's been here for five months and that's all we ever hear her say. "Back at Auburn we didn't catalog paperbacks... Back at Auburn we had blow driers in the restrooms... Back at Auburn we had evening storyhours... Back at Auburn we had C.L.S.I... Back at Auburn we had a fine amnesty every two years."

On and on and on she talks about the crummy Auburn Public Library as if it were the new Jerusalem of library science. Obviously she believes that everything we've done here during the past 33 years has been wrong, and everything they did at Auburn Public for the past 2 years they did right.

The irony of all this is that she goes nuts whenever anyone on staff says the words "but we've always done it this way here in Oakdale." But when she says, "Back at Auburn we did it this way," we have to treat her like she's the Messiah bringing us manna from the promised land. The real tragedy is that Auburn and Oakdale couldn't be more different. Auburn is an affluent suburban community in a large East Coast metropolitan area, and Oakdale is a sleepy rural community in the Midwestern farm belt.

How can we exorcize the words "Auburn Public" from our new director's vocabulary?

Sincerely,
SELMA

Dear Selma,

I feel for you. This is a little like being married to someone who talks about her ex-husband like he is God.

The unfortunate truth is that every new director who is brought in from the outside uses his or her last library as a frame of reference about how things should be done. (This by the way is a good argument for promoting from within the existing staff.)

Sometimes this frame of reference will last for three months; sometimes it will last for three years. Six months is the average. There is really very little that you can do except grit your teeth and get regular dental checkups.

Breaking in a new library director is the most difficult thing a library staff will ever be called upon to do (with the possible exception of breaking in a new library building). Good luck and pray hard.

Regards,
Will

Stupidity from On High Should Be Corrected Not Imitated

Dear Will,

When does commitment to professional ideals end and insubordination begin? In a nutshell that's my question. I am the director of a small liberal arts college library, and I have a cataloger who insists

on changing the Library of Congress prescribed subject heading of "Vietnamese Conflict" to "Vietnamese War." Our cataloger has been waging this little conflict/war for several years.

The old card catalog was his first battleground. One day it came to my attention that all the cards with the subject heading "Vietnamese Conflict" had been defaced. On each card the word "conflict" had been scratched out and the word "war" had been written above it in a messy scrawl of red ink that was made to look like dripping blood.

We promptly replaced these cards with a new set that had the proper subject heading, but two days later we discovered that they too had been defaced in exactly the same bloodcurdling manner. Over the period of the next 18 months, 9 sets of "Vietnamese Conflict" subject cards were sabotaged.

At first I thought it was the work of an outside agitator, a disaffected student or professor, but eventually I began to suspect that it was an inside job done by someone on the library staff with an ax to grind. This proved to be the case. One night, after the library had closed, I stopped into my office to finish some budget work that the college finance director needed the next day. There at the catalog was one of our catalogers with a fountain pen and a bottle of red ink.

Although surprised about being caught, this cataloger did not seem to be embarrassed about what he was doing. In fact he appeared to be rather proud of himself. He felt strongly that the L.C. subject heading was intentionally misleading. He explained that the word "conflict" connoted a short and rather insignificant skirmish between two countries. In his words what happened in Vietnam was "a full scale war" and it was the responsibility of the library to tell the truth about it. He felt strongly that the Library of Congress was being very deceitful in using the heading "Conflict."

I explained to him that whether Vietnam was a war or a conflict did not really matter to the library. The issue, I told him, was not about semantics but about conforming to the industry standards put forth by the Library of Congress. I also told him that as a professional he should understand the importance of maintaining standardized cataloging data. I explained that if libraries suddenly began to whimsically change subject headings the result would be bibliographic anarchy.

My little diatribe must have been effective because soon after that his assaults on our card catalog ceased. Two years later, however, when we went on-line, our problems began anew. Not so mysteriously, the subject heading Vietnamese Conflict was entered as Vietnamese War. As soon as I discovered this I called the cataloger into my office for another counseling session. This time he was not nearly so compliant. He told me that he would continue to enter new books under the heading of Vietnamese War. He called this an act of civil disobedience that he was morally committed to perform.

Now I don't know what to do. This man is a very good cataloger and a very good person. With the exception of his intransigence on the Vietnam issue he is a model employee. I do not want to lose him but I feel that if his insubordination continues, I will be forced to dismiss him.

Not only is the principle of cataloging uniformity at issue here, but also my authority as director is being challenged. What do you recommend that I do?

Sincerely,

EMBATTLED

Dear Embattled,

The irony here is that you are haunted by the same hobgoblins that got us into Vietnam: (1) the domino theory and (2) our obsession with our image as a superpower.

My strong advice is swallow your pride and implement a strategic retreat from your blind adherence to the principle of conforming obediently to all industry standards put forth from on high.

Changing one subject heading will not cause a domino effect in which all other subject headings will topple. Bibliographical chaos will not result if you change the word "conflict" to "war."

Also, your stature as a director will be enhanced, not diminished, if you show the ability to listen to and implement the recommendations of your staff. No one likes to work for a despot. Your flexibility is what is important here, not your authority.

Finally, your cataloger happens to be absolutely correct. What took place in Vietnam between 1961 and 1975 was war—one of the longest, costliest, and bloodiest wars in world history. It certainly is deceitful of the Library of Congress to call such carnage a "conflict." If you do not believe me take a trip to Washington, D.C., and visit the Vietnam Memorial. If you can stand in front of that wall of death and still maintain your industry standard, you need psychiatric help.

There is still another point. No one I know refers to our experience in Vietnam as a conflict. It is, therefore, not only intellectually and morally dishonest to use the L.C. heading, it is also confusing to the public.

Instead of court-martialing your cataloger, you should give him a medal.

Regards,
Will

If You Want Creative Employees, Become a Creative Interviewer

Dear Will,

I am the director of a large metropolitan public library and am currently in the process of selecting an assistant director who will have responsibility in two main areas – managing a budget of $10,000,000 and administering a staff of 300 employees.

After screening out the 112 applications that were submitted, I interviewed five finalists. Of these, two people stood out head and shoulders above the rest. The problem is I can't decide which one to hire. They are both well qualified with excellent work records and superb academic backgrounds.

What I want is someone who will be creative – an administrator who is not afraid to take risks. I don't want someone who will just go by the book even if the book is the latest claptrap from the trendiest management guru. I want someone who is creative enough to write his or her own book – one tailor made for our organization, not I.B.M. Unfortunately this is a difficult quality to determine from a résumé or a one hour office interview.

I plan to take each of the two finalists out to lunch to get to know them better. What kind of questions do you think I should ask?

Sincerely,
DOUBTFUL

Dear Doubtful,

If you're looking for a creative person, ask off-beat, unexpected questions. Most finalists competing for a high level management job are well schooled in how to handle all the obvious interview questions (How did you decide to get into librarianship, what are your strengths and weaknesses, how would you describe your management style, etc.).

What you need to do is come up with questions that they are probably not prepared to handle. Here are a few suggestions: (1) If your personality were a food what kind of food would it be? (2) If you could change one thing about the universe what would it be? (3) Name three things you like about Dan Quayle? (4) Do you think Jerry Lewis is funny or pathetic? (5) What is your ultimate library fantasy? (6) Discuss the last three books that you have read.

You might think that the last question would be strictly powder puff for a librarian but I have used it many times and have seen it strike sheer terror into the hearts of the most technically correct librarians around.

Regards,
Will

*   *   *

What's Good for the Staff Is Good for the Director

Dear Will,

Why is it that managers are so fickle? I swear the woman who runs my library must wake up every New Year's Day and make a resolution to try a new management style. She has been here seven years and we have had seven different management philosophies – (1) Zen, (2) Left Brain, (3) Cybernetics, (4) Participative, (5) Excellence, (6) Right Brain, and now something called (7) Gladiatorial. It's like she goes to "Managers R Us" and comes back with a new managerial hula hoop.

She says that this is the 90s and that cooperation is out and confrontation is in. Hence we have a new gladiatorial style. Basically a gladiatorial form of management pits one employee against another. Apparently the underlying psychological principle is that competition brings out the best in people. In the heat of battle you will supposedly find reserves of strength that you never knew you had.

Personally I think that this may have some validity if we are talking about soldiers in combat but it is pure nonsense when applied to reference librarians serving the public. Although right from the beginning I hated the thought of being pitted against my reference colleagues in some kind of a bibliographic skeet shoot, I never thought that this new hula hoop would turn into the nightmare that it has become. I figured that it would be just another passing phase to be discarded like an old Christmas tree next January 1, but our director unfortunately seems determined to stick with this one permanently.

What really bothers me is the way that it is being implemented. To make competition between employees meaningful, our pay plan has been radically changed. Instead of giving everybody "across the board" raises at the beginning of each fiscal year, we now have a "pay for performance" system that is supposed to reward the best employees and penalize the worst. In essence, employees compete with each other for pay increases.

There is an inherent problem, however, whenever a "pay for

performance" system is implemented in the public sector: it is difficult, if not impossible to determine a standard of performance by which you can separate the sheep from the goats. In the private sector this is not a problem because profit margins and sales figures are quantitatively verifiable. But there is no "bottom line" measurement by which to judge individual library employees. In the past (before the arrival of gladiatorial management) our yearly evaluations were largely impressionistic, but impressionistic observations are hopelessly subjective and thus inappropriate for determining something as important as somebody's salary.

So our beloved director has created a new and objective "hidden evaluation" system for reference librarians. This is the way it works: The director secretly has a spy call you at the reference desk with a question — for example, "What steps must you go through in pouring a foundation for a sun deck on the back of your house?" Over a period of a month each reference librarian would be asked this question by the spy. The spy would make a complete record of how each

librarian answered the question, and the answers would then be compared for accuracy and comprehensiveness. On the basis of this information the director would be able to rank order the performance of each reference librarian. This rank ordering would then serve as the basis for pay for performance.

All of us in the reference department are appalled at this snooping. Have you ever gotten undressed at night in a hotel room and felt that you were being spied on? That's the way we feel about this new method of evaluations. We feel that we are constantly being watched. We are always on edge, probably because of the paranoia we all feel whenever the phone rings. In fact, whenever the phone rings (even at home) I jump like I've been hit in the stomach.

Please help!

Sincerely,
ABOUT READY TO GO ON STRIKE

Dear Ready to Strike,

There is nothing inherently illegal about unobtrusive testing. So any thoughts of strikes, grievances, or lawsuits should be quickly forgotten.

Your only hope to get rid of this odious system is to turn the tables and do some unobtrusive evaluations of your director. Start monitoring her every move – how much time she takes for lunch, how much time she spends in the bathroom, how much time she spends at meaningless meetings – that sort of thing. Then start making phone calls of your own to her and see how she responds when as a "concerned citizen" you start questioning her about her travel and local meetings budget.

Surreptitiously turn this information over to the Board Chair in the form of an anonymously authored memo entitled, "Hidden Evaluation of Our Library Director."

I absolutely guarantee that you will be onto a new management hula hoop in no time!

Regards,
Will

*   *   *

It's Time to Take the Grocery Bags Off the Heads of Your Trustees

Dear Will,

Several months ago I got a strange request from one of my trustees. He asked me to investigate the cost of putting framed pictures of the nine members of the library board up on the wall of the lobby of the library. Let me make it clear that he was not talking about a single group picture.

At last month's board meeting I announced that the cost of the studio photography alone for the nine pictures would be in excess of $700. I was relieved that the figure was so high because I felt that this high an expense would discourage the board from approving such a bizarre request. I know of no other library that has pictures of its board members on display. That is something you would expect to see at a City Council or County Board Level where the members are elected by the people and there is a certain political advantage to getting as much public exposure as possible, but the library board is an appointive body.

To my dismay the board actually gave a great deal of serious consideration to the matter and decided to put it on the agenda for approval at next month's meeting. I am horrified. Besides spending all that money on a frill at a time when our book budget is being cut, the whole notion just seems so egregiously egotistical on their part.

Do you have any ideas about how I can stop this runaway train?

Sincerely,
JANICE

Dear Janice,

Personally I think it's a great idea! For some time I have felt that our trustees are the invisible people of our profession. This is terribly ironic because no one is more important to the future of public libraries than they are. Yet when you mention the term "library board" to the average person all you'll get in return is a blank stare.

Therefore why not give your trustees some public recognition? Why not take the grocery bags off their heads? They deserve some visibility.

Who cares if no other public libraries showcase pictures of their trustees? For once in your life you can be a trendsetter. It's just one more proof of the fact that trustees often have better judgment than directors.

Thanks for the idea, I'm going to implement it in my library right away.

Regards,
Will

Uniforms Are Meant for Century 21 Salesmen, Not Librarians

Dear Will,

One of the reasons I think that librarianship is a doormat profession is that we are such mediocre dressers. My professional staff of 12 is a very good example. The men typically wear plaid shirts with pants that have a high content of polyester, and on their feet they wear these ponderous shoes with thick rubber soles. But believe it or not they may actually be better dressers than the women, who seem to think that wearing sandals with stockings is a manifestation of a perfectly normal person.

Short of prescribing a detailed dress code, I've tried everything imaginable to get them to be more fashion conscious. I myself started beefing up my wardrobe but no one seemed to notice. Then I required them to attend a "dress for success" workshop that was sponsored by the local Chamber of Commerce. But that was like sending a horde of Hell's Angels to catechism class. It just didn't take. During the week after the workshop there was less evidence of stripes on plaids, but still there was a preponderance of polyester. It was just coordinated better.

Finally I brought in a color consultant who sat down with each

librarian and determined the best color combinations for each individual. This resulted in new colors but on the same old shiny fabrics. I really believe that some of the librarians just went out and had their existing wardrobe dyed to conform to their suggested color schemes.

I have come to the regrettable conclusion that my staff has been infected with some contagious disease that causes them all to have bad taste. Therefore I don't think a dress code will help because if I do implement "clothing guidelines" requiring coats and ties, the men will (with the best of intentions) end up wearing weird ties with weird coats.

I'm convinced that the only solution is to resort to uniforms. What I have in mind is something very basic yet very professional – nice, crisp woolen navy blue blazers with gray slacks and a burgundy tie or scarf. Requiring the staff to wear uniforms is the only way I know to make my librarians look presentable. It's ironic but many of my clerical employees dress better than the professionals.

What do you think?

Sincerely,
LINDA

Dear Linda,

My strong opinion is that uniforms are demeaning in a democratic society and no professional should be made to wear them.

Think about it. What types of people wear uniforms? That's right – waitresses, dental technicians, ticket agents, security guards, and Century 21 salesmen. I really don't think we want to be in that category.

Regards,
Will

*   *   *

A Nudist Wedding
Is a Good Way to Save
on Tuxedo and Wedding Dress Costs

Dear Will,

I know all about the recent federal court decisions about sexual harassment so you don't have to lecture me about the importance of sensitizing my employees (I'm the personnel director for a large university library) to all the various forms of sexually oriented behavior (leering, smirking, fondling, suggesting, and joking) that the courts have deemed to be inappropriate and illegal in the workplace. I know all that!

My problem deals with a man named Carl who works in acquisitions. He is a nudist. He claims that nudism works for him as a kind of religion. "Pantheism" is I think the way he describes the more spiritual aspects of nudism. This is all well and good, and certainly his freedom to worship as he pleases is protected under the First Amendment.

Each weekend Carl  drives twenty miles to commune with other nudists at a beach front nudist colony named Valhalla. He once asked me to consider joining him there for a weekend, and although I will admit to having a certain voyeuristic curiosity about the place I declined, saying, "I'm just not there yet, Carl."

Carl's nudism had never created any problems up until yesterday when he brought his wedding pictures to work and placed them on his work station in the acquisitions department. This in and of itself is not unusual. Most of our employees display some sort of family pictures either on their desk or in their office, and often if an employee has just gotten married a picture of the wedding naturally appears on top of the computer terminal or next to the telephone.

Carl's wedding pictures, however, have created more interest than most. Two weeks ago he got married at Valhalla, and the resultant photographs are filled, as you would obviously expect, with full frontal and in some cases dorsal nudity. So far, so good.

Although I was initially concerned with the appropriateness of these portraitures, upon close inspection (and I did inspect them thoroughly) I realized that the nudity was neither gender specific (there were roughly an equal number of male nudes and female nudes in the wedding party) nor prurient (there were no erotic poses). Also, I want to emphasize that this is a university library we are talking about here where you would hope that people would have more of a tolerance for cultural diversity, and furthermore, Carl's pictures were in no way accessible to library users.

So I decided that Carl's pictures (even in light of the recent court decisions about the inappropriateness of pinups) could not be construed as a form of sexual harassment. Unfortunately Muriel, one of Carl's co-workers, has filed a formal written complaint about the photos. She claims that they make her feel uncomfortable and thus they should be banned (she cited the recent court decision about pinups in the workplace).

After conversing with Carl about Muriel's complaint, I have discovered that he is not willing to take the pictures down, and his refusal is based on his First Amendment religious freedoms. He believes strongly that pictures of a nudist wedding have as much right to be displayed as pictures of a Catholic wedding.

What should I do?

Sincerely,

A HARASSED PERSONNEL DIRECTOR

Dear Harassed,

My guess is that Carl has the stronger legal case. To me intent is the key to determining what constitutes sexual harassment, and Carl's pictures are obviously not intended to titillate. People who have been to nudist colonies tell me that they are among the least erotic places you could ever imagine. "Mostly what you see is cellulite," is what one observer told me.

On the other hand, nudism does make people uncomfortable, and it does seem that Carl is being a bit of an exhibitionist to display pictures of himself and his wife naked. Think about it, wouldn't you feel uncomfortable if every time you walked past a co-worker's desk you had to look at him or her nude?

Therefore from a human dignity standpoint, I would sit down

with Carl and strongly suggest that he remove the pictures. You might explain to him that while nudist weddings have their advantages (you certainly save on tuxedo and wedding dress costs) they do have their disadvantages (not everyone wants to look at your photographs).

I hope this helps. If you want a more in-depth analysis, please send me copies of the photographs so that I can give them my first hand scutiny.

Regards,
Will

You Don't Need a Library to Find Out Where Elvis Is Hiding

Dear Will,

We are getting more and more requests from our patrons for the *National Enquirer*. It has always seemed to me that such tabloid publications are taboo in the public library and I have never given serious thought to subscribing to them. But one of my reference librarians pointed out to me yesterday that many of the nonfiction bestsellers that we stock on our book shelves are of the tabloid "true confession" ilk. For instance, in her recent autobiography *Breaking the Silence,* Mariette Hartley, the woman who appears with James Garner on the Polaroid commercials, admits to drinking vodka out of mustard jars and squatting in front of the refrigerator to eat Purina Cat Chow.

Do you feel it is hypocritical for the library not to get the *National Enquirer?*

Sincerely,
WHAT'S THE WORLD COMING TO?

Dear World,

I'll be very honest. I read the *National Enquirer* regularly. It is the perfect thing for waiting in line at the supermarket checkout counter. Its tabloid shape makes it easy to handle and its generous use of color photographs and arresting headlines ("PHONE FREAK DOG CALLS DATING LINE LONG DISTANCE") make it easy to browse through.

There is never any need to read the actual text of the articles since they give very little information that is not contained in the headlines. Consequently you can plow through an entire edition of the *Enquirer* in approximately the amount of time it takes to get your groceries checked. Also the content of the *Enquirer* is great fun. Their writers have a wonderfully ironic sense of humor. The *Enquirer* is social satire at its best.

Furthermore, it tells us a lot about America. In fact, if aliens from outer space were to ring my doorbell and ask what one publication would give them the most accurate portrayal of America would I give them *Moby Dick, The New York Times,* or *Time Magazine?* Of course not. I would give them the *National Enquirer,* the most widely circulated periodical in America.

There in living color and bold faced print are all of our innermost hopes, dreams, and fears. Just pick up any single issue and you will

see our love of money (PSYCHIC PREDICTS WINNING LOTTERY
NUMBERS AND COSTS STATE $12 MILLION), our dread of aging
(BEAUTY SECRETS FROM THE GOLDEN GIRLS), our fascination
with horror (A KILLER SHARK RIPPED MY FLESH FROM THE
BONE), our interest in the bizarre (MICHAEL JACKSON DANCES AT
VALENTINO'S GRAVE), our love of gossip (LIZ SHATTERED AS HER
GAY SECRETARY COMMITS SUICIDE), our obsession with our bodies
(PLASTIC SURGERY TURNS ORDINARY GUYS INTO BEEFY HE-
MEN; CHEST IMPLANTS MAKE THEM LOOK LIKE HUNKS), our
fondness for the grotesque (MY DATE WAS AN ANGEL TILL SHE
TURNED MY HOME INTO A RAGING INFERNO), our distrust of
government (TOWN WITHOUT PITY – HUBBY BANNED FROM PARK-
ING TRUCK IN HIS DRIVEWAY FOR 20 MINUTES TO HELP SICK
WIFE), and our fear of death (YOUR ODDS OF BEING MURDERED
WERE FAR GREATER IN THE GOOD OLD DAYS).

The *National Enquirer* is a lot like *Playboy*. Everybody rips it
publicly, but reads it privately. When you get right down to it, we *do*
want to know who JFK loved, what Cher does in her free time, and
where Elvis is hiding. But that does not mean that we should spend
public library monies to find these things out. The library has a
higher purpose than pandering to public tastes. In fact, the main
reason it exists is to offer our citizens something more substantial
and more uplifting than what is so easily encountered in grocery
store checkout lines. It is our special charge to give our taxpayers
what they can't find in the convenience stores, supermarkets, and
video stores of our communities.

And as for Mariette Hartley, I really *don't* care how much Purina
Cat Chow she has eaten in her lifetime and how much vodka she has
consumed out of a mustard jar. I disliked her as an actress and I
dislike her even more as an author. I'm sure the only reason she
wrote her book was because not even the *National Enquirer* cared
about her cat food diet.

Now if it had been Liz Taylor it would have been different. Liz is
someone we care about.

Regards,
Will

*   *   *

A Strong Library Always Has a Strong Board of Trustees; a Weak Library Always Has a Weak Board

Dear Will,

"Fussbudget" is a term that has often been applied to librarians with some justification. As a 20-year member of a public library board of trustees I am in a position to make such an observation. In my long tenure we have had five different library directors of widely varying ages, personalities, and backgrounds.

For all their differences, however, they have all had one thing in common—an inordinate concern with minute operational details. It seems to me that chief administrative officers ought to be more concerned with what President Bush has maladroitly called "the vision thing" and less concerned with which plastic cover is best suited for paperback books.

Here we are in a prosperous city of 50,000 hard working and industrious people and we have an old rinky-dinky, run-down public library that might be sufficient for a city of 5,000 people. The last library director we had, who God forbid has moved on to bigger and better things in a much larger city, was more concerned about making our bookmobile handicapped accessible than in building a new building so that handicapped individuals could actually use our main library collection.

As head of the search committee for a new director I'd welcome any advice you might be able to offer me in how to distinguish (in an interview situation) a nitpicker from a big picture person. Our library needs a leader, not another micromanager.

Sincerely,
HAROLD THE TRUSTEE

*   *   *

Dear Harold,

Good luck on the selection of a new library director. I hate to tell you this but given your attitude you will never find the miracle worker that you're so desperate to hire. Most library directors cannot pull rabbits out of hats. Magic is not a part of the A.L.A. accredited library school curriculum.

The fact is if your library is as bad as you say it is, you have no one to blame but yourself and your colleagues on the board of trustees. Library directors do not secure the funding necessary to build new library buildings. That is the responsibility of the board.

When it comes to political power, library directors are impotent. A library board of trustees, however, carries a considerable load of political capital. The trick is to use it. Trustees represent voters; library directors represent the library profession. Directors can point out the deficiencies of a given library, but they carry no sway with city councils and county commissions.

The foremost responsibility of the board of trustees is not to sign annual reports or attend library trustee conferences, it is to fight for library funding in the political arena. This means that trustees must be willing to roll up their sleeves and skin their knuckles in the sometimes rough and tumble world of local politics. Any trustee who is not willing to get a little dirty should vacate his or her seat in favor of someone who is.

It is an absolute universal truth that where you have a strong, well funded, up-to-date library, you have a strong board of trustees that knows when to flex its muscles and bare its knuckles. It is conversely true that where you find a weak, underfunded public library you will find an effete and ineffectual board.

Therefore, Harold, it is obvious to me that your problem lies not with your director but with you and the rest of your board. Your ineffective board is probably the main reason why you have had such rapid turnover in your directorship and why you have attracted weak, and small minded individuals in that position.

Even though your question about how to distinguish a visionary from a fussbudget misses the point, I'll go ahead and answer it with the hope that your board will finally develop some backbone. Just use one test – the checkbook test. Ask the candidate at what point he considers his checkbook to be balanced. Anyone who answers within a hundred dollars or more is a big picture man; anyone who answers within two dollars is a fussbudget.

This test has never failed me. Once you hire your visionary, please support him/her.

> Regards,
> Will

Underwear Awareness Is a Key to Understanding the Modern World

Dear Will,

I am a man – so by definition I only understand how half the world works. To those women who complain about men being dense, I plead guilty, very guilty. I admit it – I do not understand women. This creates problems because 23 out of the 24 people on my library staff are women.

My latest source of befuddlement stems from a phenomenon called "the lingerie party." I was introduced to the term last night when my secretary came up to me just as I was leaving the office and said, "You don't have any objections to the lingerie party that we have made plans to have in the staff lounge on Friday night after the library closes, do you?"

Now don't you just love it when somebody on your staff – especially your secretary – asks you to approve something that has been extensively planned and has practically already happened? Who but Saddam Hussein would have the courage to say no?

Nice guy that I am, I nodded my head, mumbled that it would be okay, and hurried out the door. On my way home, however, it dawned on me that I have absolutely no idea what a lingerie party is.

It's not something that I could possibly be fired for, is it? I mean it does sound a bit kinky, no? Surely it's not one of those deals with the male dancers, is it?

Will, my head is full of worries. Help me.

> Sincerely,
> PANICKED

Dear Panicked,

Breathe easy my friend. According to my secretary you're not going to get fired. She says that a lingerie party is just like a tupperware party except that they sell lace instead of plastic. Makes perfect sense, right?

But could you ever imagine a bunch of guys getting together for a Fruit of the Loom party?

Sincerely,
Will

*   *   *

A Retrospective Conversion Is to a Cataloger What a Bottle of Whiskey Is to a Drunk

Dear Will,

My beef is with the publishing industry, and it's not the usual complaint about the unfair discounts that libraries receive when compared to bookstores. My concern has to do with titles. With computerized keyword searching the need for subject headings would be completely unnecessary if only publishers would use the titles that reflect the actual subject content of the book.

For instance, Ernest Hemingway wrote an excellent nonfiction book entitled *Death in the Afternoon*. From its title you would have no idea that this book is a very comprehensive account of bullfighting in Spain. Because the title is unclear the need for subject headings is obvious. If the book were retitled *Bullfighting in Spain* it could be quickly accessed by subject with a simple keyword search. There would be no reason for the book to be assigned subject headings.

Just think of the cost savings that would result if we could only get publishers to take my idea seriously. Thousands of catalogers could be fired or at least put to more productive work at the reference desk.

Sincerely,
MYRON

Dear Myron,

Your idea is very tantalizing. Any plan that might result in the elimination of 30,000 catalogers is certainly worth considering. However, I have two main objections:

(1) Your plan will actually increase the number of catalogers on the planet. The library profession is famous for its retrospective conversions. In fact we are addicted to retrospective conversions. Why do you think catalogers keep changing their cataloging rules? So they can do retrospective conversions. The retrospective conversion is the ultimate form of job security for a cataloger.

But all of the retrospective conversions that have ever been done in the history of librarianship amount to a mere foothill compared to the mountain that would be created by retrospectively changing every title of every book ever published in order to eliminate subject headings. Try to imagine a world in which every fourth person was a cataloger. That's what would happen under your plan.

(2) My other objection is that if your plan were adopted no one would ever read a book again. A title is just as important to the success of a book as the text is. For instance would anyone read *Moby Dick* if it were retitled *Scenes from the New England Whaling Industry of the Nineteenth Century?*

Regards,
Will

God Forbid That We Would Allow Library Trustees the Right to Exercise Their Intellectual Freedoms

Dear Will,

I have been a director of a medium-sized public library located in a Midwestern town of 50,000 for seven years. During the first six years I had a cordial and constructive relationship with my board of trustees.

From time to time at various library conferences I had heard horror stories about how difficult the director-board relationship can be, but I myself had never had even the hint of a problem in that

area. My situation seemed so easy. I had my role to run the library, supervise the staff, administer the budget, provide information on policy issues, and implement board decisions. The board basically made policy and I basically made the policy happen. The board always valued my professional judgment, and I have always valued its sense of community standards. And then Sarah P. was appointed to the board, and now everything has changed and I'm one of those people you can find in the bar late at night at library conferences talking about how bad my board is.

Sarah P. is a reference librarian at the local state university. She is on a tenure track and in order to get her tenure she has to do three things: (1) stay out of trouble, (2) publish a few research articles, and (3) perform relevant community services work. Her membership on the library board fulfills her community services requirement.

But this does not give her the right to take over the control of my library. Like a lot of academic librarians she has an unstated sense of superiority around public librarians. She seems to think that because academic librarians serve an elite clientele of professors and students that makes them superior to those of us who are forced to serve street people.

Unfortunately Sarah brings her obnoxious sense of superiority to the board table. She is constantly second guessing my decisions and recommendations, and because she is a librarian the rest of the board listen to her with great respect, and the more respect they give her, the less respect they give me.

It has gotten to the point where when a policy issue arises the board looks to Sarah rather than to me for advice. Obviously my role as director has been undercut, but I am even more miffed by the fact that Sarah's influence on the rest of the board is resulting in poor policy decisions.

In short she is treating the public library like it is an academic institution and has persuaded the board to make some radical changes in the expenditures of our allotted budgetary funds. Specifically the purchase of popular books has been greatly reduced and more money has been devoted to nonfiction.

Anyone who knows anything about public libraries knows that such policies, idealistic as they are, spell doom and extinction. Public libraries are not academic libraries, no matter how much we wish they were.

Sincerely,

A LIBRARY DIRECTOR WHO NO LONGER DIRECTS

Dear Directs,

God forbid that the public library be perceived as a place of learning! I say that Sarah P. should be congratulated, not condemned, for raising basic questions about the purpose of the public library. All libraries – school, special, academic, and public – are first and foremost centers of learning, and the public library in particular is a center of lifelong learning.

You say that academic librarians look down upon public librarians. Of course they look down upon us when we abandon our role of educator in favor of a role of recreation coordinator. Libraries should be centers of education, not entertainment.

Finally in my opinion Sarah P. is not out of line from a procedural perspective. You liked your board when it functioned as a rubberstamp. But wake up. We live in a democratic society in which it is the right and privilege of the taxpayers and their duly appointed representatives to govern their public institutions.

Regards,
Will

Always Take a Swamp Over a Quagmire

Dear Will,

My board president is one of those women – and I say this as a compliment – who could be anywhere between 37 and 53. My guess is that she's closer to 53.

There is only one word that describes her properly – "stately." She carries herself well. She is tall, has perfect posture, and she's got her hair (more salt than pepper) spiraled up on top of her head in a perfect circular pattern. Also, her jewelry is definitely top of the line stuff – no junk, no faux pearls, no baubles, no bangles, no dangles – it's all diamonds and gold, but understated, very understated. And she's as thin as a carrot stick, which as far as I can tell, is basically all that she eats.

Put her in a black dress, black stockings, and black pumps and you've got an Audrey Hepburn clone. At times she seems more like a fine piece of china than a member of the human race, but you know that she's not completely unflawed because there's the slightest of scars just above her left eyebrow like someone hit her with a stone there when she was a little kid.

Like a lot of skinny people, however, she's an absolute circuit board of nerves and nervous energy. I'm talking about the kind of person who's always dotting your i's, crossing your t's, and completing your sentences because you don't talk fast enough. She's definitely a woman on the go – a real estate agent who only handles houses in the quarter of a million dollar and up category that are located in "desirable neighborhoods," as if someone's going to build a quarter of a million dollar house in an undesirable neighborhood.

If you can get her to turn off the high tech beeper that she keeps in her designer leather beeper holder, she is – and I hate to use this word – a rather dynamic board president. I mean there's no way I could have ever gotten the city council on my own to approve a resolution authorizing a citizens' vote on the question of financing a new main building. Alicia's help was indispensable. She proved to be a master political operative who knew just what button to push for each councilperson.

But more important than that, she masterminded the referendum campaign that resulted in the library bond issue passing by a three to one margin, a near miracle when you consider that the previous three library referendums failed miserably.

Alicia and I subsequently got a lot of national notoriety for the article that we wrote entitled, "Getting a Bond Referendum Passed When You Have Neither Hope Nor Money." As a result of this attention we became a hot commodity on the library speaking circuit. It seemed like every state and regional trustee association in the country wanted us to do seminars, workshops, and consultations, and so we began spending a lot of time together on the road.

Before all of this traveling started, our relationship could best be described as businesslike. There wasn't much small talk between us, and we never conversed about personal issues – mainly because Alicia was too busy for that sort of thing. On our speaking trips, however, there was time to chat and our relationship began to warm up, not that we ever became chummy.

There was still a polite distance between us, but the distance had closed enough for Alicia to start making a certain little request that at first I tried to laugh off and then later ignore. But now it's gotten to the crisis stage and I NEED HELP.

Here's the deal: Alicia wants me to fire Sandra, the head of my children's department, because Sandra's father stiffed Alicia on a real estate deal that she set up for him seven years ago. Knowing that he worships the ground that Sandra walks on, Alicia figures that canning Sandra would be just revenge. Makes a lot of sense, right?

Over and over I've told Alicia that there is simply no way under the law that I can fire Sandra. Furthermore I've told Alicia that putting all legalities aside, I have some real ethical qualms about arbitrarily dismissing someone who is an exemplary employee.

To my chagrin, however, I've discovered that the nasty little details of public personnel law mean absolutely nothing to people like Alicia who work in the private sector. They think that they can fire anybody they want whenever they want. So we have had this on-going disagreement that gives our relationship an undesirably sharp edge.

Now I've made a terrible mistake. On the flight to the Southeastern Trustees Association Conference in Tampa our DC 10 went into rapid descent, which means that for about twenty terrifying seconds, it looked very much like we were going to crash into the middle of a swamp in Georgia. Fortunately, our pilot regained control of the airplane and things returned to normal. I, however, was so stressed out that when I got up to go to the bathroom I forgot to lock the little door, which was very stupid because two minutes later Alicia opened the door and voilà – there I was sitting on the little toilet. . . snorting a line of cocaine. Boom, just like that I was caught.

Do you think Alicia was upset? Do you think she cared enough about me to give me the standard line about getting help? Think again. All she said to me was, "If you don't fire Sandra, I'm going straight to the Mayor and City Council about your little habit and you'll be history."

Bottom line is that Alicia has given me a month to fire Sandra. Based on all that I've told you about Alicia what would you suggest I do? What do you think are her potential weaknesses? Do you think I should hire a private detective to trail her for potential counter-blackmail material?

Sincerely,
UP A CREEK WITHOUT A PADDLE

P.S. I only use cocaine at times of severe stress, like right after rapid airplane descent!

Dear Creek,

Throw in the towel. Your options are all bad. Like most cocaine junkies you refuse to look at your situation realistically. There is no way out. Alicia is not the kind of person who leaves herself open to blackmail. As you say she's pretty flawless and she knows what buttons to push.

So get yourself a life. You need to resign your position, get into rehab, and spend some time looking at sunsets when you're finally all cleaned up. Personally, I'm not betting on your future. I predict that eventually you will regret that your DC 10 didn't end up in that swamp in Georgia because that's got to be preferable to the quagmire you're in now.

Rots of Ruck,
Will

Before You Pick a Lover Consider the Health Risks

Dear Will,

My front lawn is composed of a relatively delicate strain of bermuda tiff called Santa Anna (so when I talk to my lawn I always call it Anna for short). The truth is I love my lawn. It is the joy of my life. It is my pet, my love, my life's work.

Many people think of their lawn as a necessary evil, just another aspect of home ownership – like storm windows and leaky faucets – that requires time, money and maintenance. These people are sad. They have no harmony in their souls. They see their lawn in terms of millions of single blades of grass that need to be fertilized, sprinkled, cut, edged, and trimmed.

But to me a lawn is not a million blades of grass, it is a single, unique, organic living being with its own special needs and personality. Anna has given me so much happiness and pleasure that when I cut and trim her lush and lovely tresses I do not feel like I am working. I feel like I am making love to a beautiful woman.

Don't get me wrong, I love my wife. But the truth is she is aging and wrinkling. On the other hand, Anna stays eternally young. Obviously my wife resents all the time I spend manicuring Anna but I tell her that she's lucky that my mistress is a lawn and not the woman next door who unhooks the top of her bathing suit every afternoon at 1:37 while sunning herself in the back yard.

Actually Anna is more than a mistress. We are such soulmates that it pains me to have to leave her each morning to go to work. I'm the head of adult services for a community college library. One morning last month as I was walking into the library it suddenly dawned on me that my life didn't have to have that pain. That was the day that I noticed that a small square of earth (forty feet by forty feet) in front of the library would be much more attractive if it were grassed in. Naturally I saw it as the perfect place for Anna's first offspring.

Yesterday I told the college's director of grounds and maintenance about my idea of nurturing a lush green lawn in that space in front of the library. My concept was to create a kind of outdoor lyceum where students could gather together to eat lunch and talk about the universe. Unfortunately this glorified groundskeeper was not impressed. He told me very coldly that it was the policy of the college to eliminate grassy areas, not encourage them.

Do you think I should pursue my idea to a higher level? I am not doing this for my own selfish reasons. While it is true that I do miss Anna during the days that I have to work, I am also interested in sharing her beauty with others.

What do you think?

Sincerely,
HARVEY

Dear Harvey,

While I have never had any sexual fantasies about a lawn, I do appreciate the cool and luxurious pleasures of grass. Unfortunately, recent studies show that common lawn pesticides, herbicides, and fertilizers are poisonous and can kill children and other living things.

So your mistress may be a killer.

Sincerely,
Will

When in Doubt
Hide Behind the Library Board

Dear Will,

A local family planning organization that is dedicated to the concept of birth control and safe sex is putting a lot of pressure on me (the director of the public library) to put condom vending machines into our public restrooms. This group is not just targeting the library. They have made a similar request to other public agencies and institutions in the community. It is part of their "Education and Access" campaign.

While I understand that the goals of this organization are quite laudable, I also realize that the presence of condom machines in the restrooms of our small-town Midwestern library will be quite objectionable to a number of citizens on both religious and moral grounds. For that reason, it is my decided preference to deny the request.

Unfortunately the members of the family planning group are filled with the zeal of people who are out to do good and save humanity. They want to stop unwanted pregnancies and halt the spread of AIDS, and they will simply not take "no" for an answer. They feel that somehow this is a First Amendment issue.

What do you think I should do?

Sincerely,
HENRY

Dear Henry,

I have just reviewed the First Amendment and it speaks of freedom of press, religion, and assembly; but nowhere does it mention anything about freedom to put condoms in the restroom of the public library.

My own response in this case, therefore, would be to tell the group "no" and then to advise them of their right to appeal this decision to the library board of trustees. This is a perfect example of where the board can come in very handy to the director. It is the board's job to represent the community, and this is a perfect case of an issue that has everything to do with community standards and nothing to do with the principles of librarianship. It therefore is an issue that finally must be handled by the board.

So you're off the hook.

Regards,
Will

If Your Dinner Companions Get Out Their Calculators in Five Star Restaurants, Ask for a Doggy-Bag

Dear Will,

One of the things that I like about attending an A.L.A. convention is that it gives me the opportunity to dine at some very special

restaurants. Thanks to A.L.A. I have eaten at Bookbinders in
Philadelphia, Amelio's in San Francisco, and Spago in Los Angeles. I
consider those experiences to be educational and cultural adventures
and well as culinary treats. Unfortunately the pleasure of those even-
ings has often been spoiled by the conduct of my librarian dining
companions.

At each A.L.A. conference there are always five or six of us who
get together to share ideas, catch up on gossip, and go out to a fancy
restaurant. Everything goes well until the bill arrives. Then out
come the dueling calculators, and I just want to crawl under the
table from embarrassment.

I have talked to my friends about how gauche this practice is,
but they think I am too self-conscious. They add that it is the fault of
the restaurant for not writing up separate checks for each of us!

Each year I vow never to go out with these librarians again, but
except for the calculators, I always have a good time.

Do you have any suggestions? These people are my friends and going out with them is an important tradition.

> Sincerely,
> SYLVIA

Dear Sylvia,

Start a new tradition. Next time when the calculators come out, ask the maître d' for a doggy-bag and stick it over your head. Let's hope your friends get the message.

> Sincerely,
> Will

Always Dance with the One That Brung You

Dear Will,

Let's face it, golf is not a librarian's game. In fact with the possible exception of the A.L.A. Fun Run, it would be hard to associate the library profession with any type of athletic endeavor. My question for you, therefore, probably breaks new ground in the area of library etiquette.

First some background: six months ago I was hired as the assistant director for a medium-sized public library that serves a population of over 150,000 people in a Midwestern suburban community. My director fancies himself a golfer, and his office is full of golfing knick-knacks. During my interview with him, while I was stumbling over a question about the pros and cons of turnkey systems, my eye caught sight of a paperweight made from the face of a putter. "How clever," I exclaimed, picking up the paperweight.

"Do you really like it?" he asked in a very flattered tone.

"Yes, very much," I said and then added, "I'm an avid golfer myself."

"That's fantastic!" he gushed. "I've been looking for someone on staff to play golf with but there just don't seem to be any librarians interested in the game." Five minutes later I was hired.

The trouble is that this man is a terrible golfer. I know this because I'm pretty much expected to play with him every Wednesday afternoon. This is what he calls our "weekly administrative meeting." The rest of the staff resents this time that we spend on the golf course and I must say I am beginning to dread it also.

Like most men, my director has a very inflated view of his own athletic prowess. In a word his golf game is atrocious. A successful outing for him is not killing anyone either with a misdirected shot or an errant golf club. He is the worst golfer on the face of the earth.

Correct that, I am the worst golfer on the face of the earth. That's because every Wednesday afternoon he beats me decisively. But at least I have an excuse – I let him win. The truth is I am not a great golfer but the first time we played I made the mistake of beating him by twenty shots. As a result he didn't talk to me for seven whole days. Then I let him win, and his attitude toward me warmed significantly.

Now I have let him win for 18 straight weeks and he thinks that I am the greatest thing to hit the library profession since Isadora Gilbert Mudge. In fact I have already gotten two hefty pay raises. This is all well and good and I certainly have no intentions of giving up the raises but I do wish that they were for my excellence as a librarian and not for the atrocities I have perpetrated on the golf course.

The bottom line is that I am beginning to have some ethical qualms about letting him win. Besides being deceitful, this whole charade is unfortunately feeding his obnoxious sense of male supremacy. I can't stand losing to him anymore. In golf they always say play it where it lies, well I'm not sure I can continue to live this lie.

Sincerely,
AMY

*   *   *

Dear Amy,

You started this whole thing at your interview by deflecting a question away from computers and toward the subject of golf. It was a clever ploy that got you the job. At the time you didn't seem to have any ethical qualms.

There's an old expression that's relevant here—"You gotta dance with the one that brung you." If golf is what got you the job, then golf is what is going to keep the job for you.

You'll have to learn to live with that or find another job.

Sorry,
Will

The Best Things in Life— Chocolates and Lovers—Are Not Meant to Be Shared

Dear Will,

One of the nice things about our library director is that throughout the year he does the little, thoughtful things that make a big difference in staff morale. For instance, he sends a personalized card to each of us on our birthday. Also his "Great American Staff Luncheons" (hamburgers before Memorial Day, hot dogs before the Fourth of July, and barbequed chicken before Labor Day) are quite popular.

But most of all we appreciate and look forward to his candy drops. Right before Christmas, Valentine's Day, and Easter he gives each library department a five pound box of very high quality chocolates. If there is anyone in the world who does not appreciate fine chocolate, that person is obviously a mutant. Unfortunately, although we all like the chocolates he gives us, there are some people on staff who abuse these wonderful gifts. This bothers me and I know that it bothers others.

There are four types of chocolate abusers on staff: (1) Pigs—
These people need Betty Ford type help. They are unabashed
chocoholics who cannot stop at one, two, or three pieces of chocolate.
Alfred is probably our most serious addict. I have seen him eat as
many as eight pieces of fine, rich, and expensive chocolates in less
than 75 seconds.

(2) Squirrels—These people, like the pigs, make repeated trips to
the chocolate box, but unlike the pigs, they squirrel the candy away
in their desk drawers (often in catalog card boxes). Two weeks after
all the chocolates are gone they love to make a public display of how
much they are still enjoying the director's Christmas candy. This is
particularly upsetting to those of us who have made New Year's
resolutions to lose weight.

(3) Hummingbirds – These are the people who are just too fit and trim. You hate them so much that you tend to spread rumors that they are anorexic or bulimic. They love to buzz around the chocolate box during the holiday season and make public pronouncements about the exact number of calories in each piece of candy. All the while they conspicuously show off their ability to eat nothing more fattening than a piece of celery or a carrot stick.

(4) Gerbils – Have you ever watched a gerbil eat? There's a lot of nervous poking and probing that goes on before a gerbil actually puts any food into his mouth. I absolutely hate the people who poke a piece of chocolate to see what is inside of it, and if their poking does reveal something undesirable they put the now dented piece of chocolate back in the box. Who then wants to eat a piece of chocolate that's been handled and poked?

The chocolate abusers are making the gift a source of bitterness and frustration rather than a source of cheer and goodwill.

What can be done about this?

Sincerely,
SUE

Dear Sue,

I myself am a chocolate lover, and I too have seen the types of abuse that you have experienced. Call me a pessimist about the human race, but based on all my experiences – both at the library and at home – the concept of more than two people sharing a box of chocolates seems hopelessly unrealistic.

Chocolate does funny things to people. It makes nice people greedy, charitable people selfish, and outgoing people secretive. Chocolate is not like a watermelon. It simply cannot be shared.

My advice is that your director give each employee a little box of candy. Chocolate is a very personal thing that should be eaten in the privacy of one's own home.

Regards,
Will

*   *   *

Never Accept a Paperweight from an Old Man Unless You're Willing to Go to the Bahamas with Him

Dear Will,

I work the reference desk 35 hours a week in a medium sized public library. During the six years that I have worked for this library I have gotten to know a good number of our regular patrons on a first name basis.

Oscar is such a patron. He is a lonely old man (70-something) who comes in and chats every Friday morning. Over the years he has developed a special liking for me because I always make it a point to save the library's newest murder mysteries for him. He has a passion for whodunits and has read every single one in our collection at least twice.

In the past three months, however, there has been a perceptible change in our relationship. He has been bringing me presents. At first they were rather innocent—a knick-knack for my desk, tickets to the circus, an African violet, some chocolates—that sort of thing. Lately, however, they have been getting more and more expensive. Three weeks ago he gave me a beautiful designer sweater and last Friday he gave me an exquisite golden necklace.

But the most upsetting thing is that he has begun talking about taking me on a Caribbean cruise. I am single and Oscar is a darling man, but I am 28 and have no interest in him other than as a pet library patron. I feel that I need to return the sweater and necklace and set him straight about our relationship but I just don't want to break Oscar's heart.

Do you know of a delicate way for me to do this?

Sincerely,
SAMANTHA

Dear Sam,

The moment that you accepted that very first gift, the knick-knack for your desk, you violated Manley's First Law of Librarian Ethics—Never Accept Any Gift from Anybody for Professional Services Rendered.

I don't care if the gift is from a book salesman, a computer vendor, a dirty old man, or a dashing young man, you should not accept it. I don't care if the gift is worth $2 or $200, you should not accept it. I don't care if it is given with the best of intentions or the worst of intentions, you should not accept it.

When you accept a gift for professional services, you are sending a message. The message you think you are sending (gratitude and appreciation) is often not the message that the giver receives. The giver will receive the message that he or she wants to receive.

If you accept a gift from a vendor, the vendor will think this means you are indebted to him and that you are committed to buying his product. He thinks he has bought you off. Never give a vendor that impression. Never accept his gifts, not even lunch, not even wine and cheese. Not even a calendar.

If you accept a gift from a kindly old man, the kindly old man will think this means you are in love with him, and soon he'll be fantasizing about hauling you off on a Caribbean cruise. It's much easier to say no at the beginning than later on.

So... Just say no! It's not too late. Unless of course you don't mind going to the Caribbean with Oscar. According to *Cosmopolitan Magazine* older men do have their charms.

Sincerely,
Will the Grinch

Human Diversity Is Wonderful; Individual Eccentricity Is Not

Dear Will,

I have always appreciated the diversity of the human family. Wouldn't it be utterly devastating to live in a world where everyone

looked the same, acted the same, and thought the same? One of the
main reasons I got into public library work was because we deal with
the entire scope of humanity – everybody from buttoned down
bankers to fat old ladies wearing muumuus. Socioeconomic levels be
damned! Respectability be damned! Conformity be damned! I don't
care if your skin is purple and your mother wears combat boots –
you're still a child of God, and as such you're my brother or sister. I
may not love you, but I'll always respect you even if you do wear
black nylon socks with your plaid bermuda shorts. And if I'm working the reference desk I'll help you with whatever inane question you
may have. Remember the only dumb questions are the ones that you
don't ask. So ask. Just don't come into my office now that I've been
promoted to assistant director. Visiting me out at the reference desk
is fine – that's where the action is, but hanging out in my offiice is not
going to do a lot for my time management or my image or the at-
mospherics in my office. I'm a busy person now and I can't afford to
while away my day chewing the fat with you. Also, I don't want my
director getting the impression that you're my best friend. And
third, you most impress me as needing a bath. To wit you make my
office stink, which is fine except that's where I live now.

Will, that's what I want to say to Mr. Sturdivant, my local library eccentric. He's an interesting guy and is the only person I know who understands Stephen Hawking's theories about the origin of the universe. But he is weird, he does stink, and a conversation with him is a time intensive matter. The problem is now that I have been promoted and have an office he just walks in and camps out— almost every other day. I have to get control of this situation. At the reference desk I could always count on a ringing phone or a patron in need of help to liberate me from his clutches. As an assistant director I no longer have those handy interruptions. Please hlep!

Sincerely,

**INTERESTED IN THE ORIGIN OF THE UNIVERSE
BUT NOT AT THE EXPENSE OF A STINKY OFFICE**

Dear Stinky Office,

This is where an alert and supportive secretary can be of great help. I once had a problem like yours. The eccentric who enjoyed camping in my office was a man named Fritz the Nazi. Fritz would expound for hours on his theories about man and the territorial imperative, an interesting topic to be sure but one that I got tired of after 30 or 40 minutes (especially since Fritz had an annoying habit of spitting while he conversed). He also believed that Lyndon Johnson was part of the conspiracy that killed President Kennedy.

Out of desperation I told my secretary, Ginnie, to always call me on the phone two minutes after Fritz had been in my office and inform me that there was a crisis in the cataloging department that needed my immediate attention (a misplaced comma or something). This stratagem was always successful in getting him out of my hair. Eventually he stopped coming around altogether.

I too love human diversity, but hey, we all have a job to do.

Regards,
Will

*   *   *

A Beep in Time Saves Nine

Dear Will,

Unlike a lot of executive secretaries, I harbor none of the usual resentments toward my boss, the library director. He's a good man who works hard and treats me very fairly. He deserves every penny he earns, and he pays me a very fair wage. I am happy.

Well, actually there is one thing I need your help on. I haven't figured out which, but my boss suffers either from acute constipation or diarrhea. This is obvious from the inordinate amount of time that he spends in the bathroom. I know this because the men's room is right down the hall from my work station and I can see when he goes in and when he comes out.

Personally I do not like to make judgments about people. If my boss ever asked me what I thought about his bathroom habits I would definitely tell him to seek medical help for whatever it is that gets him in there so frequently and keeps him in there so long. But he has never asked, and I don't like sticking my nose in his business. Furthermore we don't have the kind of relationship whereby I can give him my unsolicited advice about a matter so personal.

Don't get me wrong. The issue here is not about him idling away valuable work time. The fact is that my boss does not waste a lot of work time on his bathroom excursions. Quite the contrary. That is the place where he seems to be most productive. I have never seen him go in there without a pad and a pencil and have never seen him come out without at least one newly written memo and sometimes two and even three.

The problem is that it gets embarrassing when he gets phone calls (his phone is constantly ringing) and I have to tell the caller that he is away from his desk and the caller then asks me where he can be reached. I can't just say "the bathroom." So I say, "I really don't know where he is" which makes me look stupid and makes him look irresponsible.

But that scenario is just the tip of the iceberg. The real problem occurs when Mr. Baldwin, the president of the library board, calls and demands that I track him down right away. Mr. Baldwin is very demanding. He is the president of a local plastics company and he hates being put on hold.

So in that case I have to fetch Jimmy Heller out of acquisitions and send him into the men's room to fetch my boss. This is demeaning to me, Jimmy Heller, and my boss.

Do you have any suggestions of how I could handle this problem with greater grace and dignity?

Sincerely,
HILDA

Dear Hilda,

First of all it is my expert medical opinion that there is nothing physically wrong with your boss. His bathroom visits would appear to be prompted by a deep felt need to get away from the phone. You would be surprised at how difficult it is to get paperwork done and memos written in an office. There are constant interruptions and annoyances from a constantly ringing phone to a steady stream of visitors to a squeaky chair. The men's room represents a haven of peace, quiet, and solitude for your boss. It is no coincidence that he is so productive in there.

What he obviously doesn't realize is that his bathroom trips place you in situations of awkwardness. My advice would be to get him a beeper. Even if he is philosophically opposed to beepers on general principles, he might at least be willing to wear one to the bathroom especially when you tell him about Mr. Baldwin's chronic impatience.

I hope this helps.

Sincerely,
Will

*   *   *

Beware of the Man Who Tells You That Your Ugly Tie Is "Artistic"

Dear Will,

I am a simple man.

To me life is very clear. It is a war – a constant struggle between good and evil.

People who say that the world is gray are cowards. The world is black and white. There's right and there's wrong and there's nothing in between.

I count myself as a force for good. I am on the side of righteousness. I am a soldier of Christ. Jesus said that he did not come to bring peace but a sword. I carry that sword each and every day, and with that sword I slash and cut; maim and kill. And then I burn my victims.

I am a solitary man. I do my work alone in the shadows of darkness. Outwardly I am a most pleasant fellow. I will hold the door for you, I will tell you that your ugly tie is "artistic," and I will prate on about all manner of nonsense so that you will like me. But inwardly I burn with rage. It is true, I am an angry man, and if I hate you, I am a dangerous man.

But, alas, I am also an insignificant man. I am the lowliest of God's servants. I am a circulation clerk in a public library. I make four dollars and fifty cents an hour. I am not complaining. The money is enough to sustain me in my mission. It keeps me alive to cut and slash; maim and kill; and then to burn.

In this den of thieves and adulterers that they call a library I am one of the holy ones. I am God's mole—an undercover agent in the service of the Almighty. At the behest of the Master I faithfully unsheathe my sword—a crucifix whose tip I have honed so sharply that I can sever even the stiffest spine with it. It is my weapon of choice—the tool I use to wage my war.

My first day at the circulation desk was a revelation. At first I was appalled at the filth that I was expected to check out and then check in, but soon I realized that God had special plans for me. He had put me behind that big black granite counter for a purpose. I was to become his AVENGING CENSOR.

For seven years now I have very systematically but very secretly cut and stabbed and slashed and torn and burned over 1700 books, books full of filth that corrupt both the young and the old. James Joyce, William Faulkner, Ernest Hemingway, Philip Roth, and Norman Mailer are just a few of my victims.

And no one has caught me! I am almost disappointed. I would welcome the opportunity to publicly defend my righteousness. For seven years I have taken books home, cut them up with my crucifix, burned them, and not once have I ever been suspected. In fact, in my yearly evaluations I am always treated with praise. I am considered a most cooperative fellow. Once I was even offered a promotion as an assistant to the reference librarians but I refused. My divine calling is circulation, which is fine with my supervisor because she likes the way I smile all the time.

BUT SHE DOES NOT KNOW WHY I SMILE. BEWARE, THE END-TIME IS COMING. ARE YOU READY?

Sincerely,
GOD'S MOLE

Dear Mole,

Am I ready? Apparently not – I haven't burned any books lately. Before you take it completely for granted that you've got a reserved seat in God's inner circle in heaven, you might check out the seventh commandment. You might have trouble getting past St. Peter with that one. By my reckoning, 1700 books at $26 apiece (the average price of a library book with processing costs factored in) comes to over $44,000. That's what your private little mission has cost the taxpayers. You call it righteousness; I call it stealing. But you can take that little matter up with God at the appropriate time. Good luck.

Now let's talk some theology. Open your Bible to Genesis, and the little story about Adam, Eve, the serpent, and the tree of knowledge. I leave you with one question: If God is such a big censor why did he give us access to the tree of knowledge?

Yours in the Service of the Master,
Father Will

Do Not Give Dogs What Is Holy

Dear Will,

Single – no husband, no kids, no ex-husbands, no ex-kids – that's me – single. Always was and always will be. Men are fine for going to dinner, the symphony, a movie, a play, and even to the ballet, but they are not fine for sharing house and home. All of my friends are married, and all of my friends are miserable. I alone am happy, and I alone am single.

I am a reference librarian in a university library. My best friend is a cataloger named Anna. Anna has been married three times and divorced three times. She is an incurable romantic. We carpool together and on her car stereo she is always playing those lush romantic songs that Linda Ronstadt recorded with the Nelson Riddle Orchestra back in the 80s before Nelson Riddle died – things like "I've Got a Crush on You" and "Crazy He Calls Me." It drives me crazy.

Now Anna's decided that she's getting married again, this time to an English professor named Leo. "It's the real thing," she insists. "Leo and I are not just attracted to each other physically; we're soulmates." Of course Anna said that before marrying husbands number two and three. I didn't know her when she got married the first time.

One of the things that can happen to you when you get married a lot is that you can end up with a bunch of kids. Anna has five children. "Can I help it," she declares, "if all my husbands were oriented toward the birth experience?"

What bothers me about this is not just that Anna is the world's worst parent (she actually lets her kids watch MTV) but she gets such a big tax break for being the world's worst parent. Even though our salaries are identical, Anna's take home pay is 30 percent higher than mine because of all her dependents.

This unfairness is further compounded by the fact that she gets five times the fringe benefits that I get by virtue of the fact that all five of her children are fully covered by the university's preferred provider medical insurance policy. The other thing that burns me up is that everytime Anna has a baby she's allowed to take a four month maternity leave. No doubt she'll be getting more time off as soon as Leo decides that he wants to give her a new birth experience opportunity.

The unfairness of being single in a married and divorced world has begun to bother me to the point where I am now seriously considering making a formal request that my two dogs – Murf and Hurf – be insured under the university's medical policy.

My reasons for this request are, I think, rather compelling. For one thing, Murf and Hurf are quite healthy – much healthier in fact than Anna's five kids who are always coming down with something dreadfully contagious that invariably sweeps through the entire family like a forest fire and causes hundreds of dollars of medical bills to be charged to the university.

For another thing, Murf and Hurf are as much a part of my family as Anna's kids are a part of her family. They give me warmth, friendship, and companionship, and I truly love them both. Although Murf and Hurf are for the most part the absolute picture of health, their veterinary upkeep and health maintenance program is not altogether insignificant. Just like Anna's children, they require periodic vaccinations, check-ups, and treatments. Also I have been noticing lately that Murf seems somewhat depressed and withdrawn. He may well be having a mid-life crisis. If this is the case a few sessions with a reputable doggie psychiatrist would not hurt. When your dog's depressed, you can get very depressed also.

In closing I feel it is time that society begin recognizing the rights of single people. Much has been done over the past thirty years to help right the wrongs of discrimination against women, blacks, gays, and the handicapped. The time is ripe for a singles liberation movement.

Sincerely,
DEMI

Dear Demi,

Although more and more social commentators are attacking the many injustices that are perpetrated on single people, I have yet to see any convincing arguments linking medical insurance for pets with singles' rights.

Pet owning cuts across all racial, gender, and lifestyle lines. Owning a pet is simply not a function of being single. In fact I would be willing to bet that Anna has a menagerie of her own.

Furthermore, you're looking for advice from the wrong man. I detest the time, money, and attention that we Americans shower upon every four legged creature from the lowliest gerbil to the noblest Great Dane. A significant part of our population is hungry and malnourished and yet we spend billions of dollars on dog food.

As insufferable as Anna's children may be, they are infinitely more precious than your smelly and apparently neurotic dogs. If I can get personal, you say you are happy because you are single, and yet your attachments to Murf and Hurf border on the psychotic.

Maybe you're the one who needs to see a shrink.

Best Regards,
Will

Real Men Don't Complain About Their Image

Dear Will,

I am depressed and I know that I shouldn't be depressed. I love my job as a reference librarian and I wouldn't trade it for any other job on the face of the earth. There's nothing I would rather do than be a reference librarian. And that oddly enough is my problem.

As long as I am a reference librarian (which is probably for the rest of my life) I will get no respect from women unless Arnold Schwarzenegger suddenly reveals that his secret fantasy is to be a librarian. Until that unlikely day comes I'll continue to strike out with the opposite sex. Women are just not ready for the concept of a male librarian.

As soon as I tell a woman that I am a librarian, I can see it in her eyes that she thinks I'm a wimp, and unfortunately wimpiness is as out-moded as PeeWee Herman. I've almost decided that if I am ever going to have a serious relationship with a woman I have to either lie about my occupation or quit it altogether.

What woman is going to go out with a male librarian? Oh, I know what you are going to say—a lot of male librarians end up marrying female librarians. But for me the idea of marrying a female librarian is only slightly more palatable than marrying a female impersonator.

Advice?

Sincerely,
UNLOVED

Dear Unloved,

If you want to be a real man go out and be a real man – eat red meat, grow hair on your chest, buy a pick-up truck, chew tobacco, drink straight tequila, and kick your dog. But above all stop whining!

Regards,
Will

*   *   *

Service Equity Begins at Home

Dear Will,

Six months ago, Jean, the supervisor of my reference department, began going to night school at the local state university in pursuit of a master's degree in public administration. As part of her curriculum she is currently taking a course called "Bureaucracy 207" in which she was introduced to a concept called "service equity."

Service equity, from what I can tell, is one of those idealistic notions that in theory sounds wonderful but in practice simply does not work. According to Jean, service equity means that you give the same level of service to the panhandler off the street as you give to the mayor and members of the city council. Jean's professor feels that most governmental services are unfairly biased toward the rich and powerful. As a consequence, the rich get richer and the poor get poorer. Naturally in the professor's eye this is not right, and it is therefore the responsibility of government workers to take it upon themselves to make sure that governmental services are delivered in a fair and equitable fashion.

Unfortunately Jean is not the average student. Instead of simply snoozing her way through this course like everyone else, she has to be the one to take this pointy-headed professor and his fuzzy-wuzzy social philosophies seriously. Just yesterday the mayor called the reference department for the exact wording of a Will Rogers quote that he intended to use in a speech he was scheduled to give that night. Even though he needed the quote right away, Jean told him that he would have to wait because there were four walk-in patrons and two phone callers ahead of him.

This, of course, prompted immediate calls from the mayor to the president of the library board to me, which meant that I had to go down to the reference desk to verify the blasted quote, which I did in less than sixty seconds. At least the mayor was satisfied if not happy.

Later that afternoon I called Jean into my office to discuss the service priorities of the library. That's when she told me about her professor's theory of service equity and her own newfound commitment to social, economic, and political justice.

Do you have any practical advice for deprogramming a starry-eyed graduate student? The irony of this whole thing is that Jean gets reimbursed by the library for her tuition payments, which means that we pay her to go to school to get brainwashed. Why does she have to be so blasted intense? Why can't she play the academic game like everyone else?

Sincerely,
CYNTHIA

Dear Cynthia,

Personally, I wouldn't fool around. I would simply introduce Jean to another economic concept which is commonly called "unemployment."

Explain to her that if the mayor and members of the city council are not happy with the library, their support for library services will dwindle. This will mean that budget cuts will have to be made, and that her position may very well be among those cut.

I am confident that she will see service equity in an entirely different light.

Regards,
Will

The Best Way to Communicate with a Wayward Children's Librarian Is with a Scary Story

Dear Will,

At times I think that my children's librarian, Miss Prosch, has been at it too long. It's becoming more and more obvious that she needs a breather from the stresses and strains of working with kids.

The problem is that she is what you would call an institutional fixture, as much a part of the library as the bookstacks and study

tables. For thirty years she has held court in the basement children's room, and since our building is one of those old Carnegie models that has a separate entrance and exit to the children's room (Carnegie, God bless him, obviously felt that children should be neither seen nor heard), she has pretty much ruled her own roost down there with little interference from above.

To her credit I have to admit that her story hours are rather famous in a "local color" kind of way. She has a very theatrical narrative style and thirty years' worth of unique props that she has fashioned out of her own very creative hands. Mothers and fathers who remembered Miss Prosch from their childhoods are now bringing their own kids to the library so that they can experience her unique style of spinning a story hour. In our age of television and videogames, Miss Prosch can be positively mesmerizing.

But lately, as her library director, I have begun hearing complaints that she is scaring the children by threatening to make dumpster children of them if they misbehave. Apparently Miss Prosch has
created a whole series of gruesome stories about all the bad boys and
girls whom she has banished to the library dumpster where they live
on kitchen scraps and wail unceasingly for their parents.

These dumpster stories are made even more terrifying by the
fact that the aging process has not been kind to Miss Prosch. Let's
put it this way — with each passing day she looks more and more like
the Wicked Witch of the West.

My dilemma is obvious. Miss Prosch is a town legend. If I pull
her out of the children's library I no doubt will be seen by our
townsfolk as a local Charles Manson, and if I leave her down there I
will end up causing scores of local children to hate their hometown
library.

The bottom line is that this appears to be a lose-lose situation.
Can you help?

Sincerely,

A DIRECTOR WHO WOULDN'T MIND
HIDING IN THE DUMPSTER

Dear Dumpster Director,

You haven't given me Miss Prosch's age, but I'll hazard the guess
that she is near or even past a normal retirement age, and therefore
my strong advice is that you need to retire her, a very tricky task
that can result in your own premature retirement if you handle it
incorrectly.

In a nutshell you must make retirement seem like her idea. The
worst thing you can do is make her feel that you are pressuring her
to leave. This will create bad feelings that will cast you in a very bad
light in front of the entire community. The problem with this approach is that it sounds good in theory but is impossible to implement in practice. So stop dreaming that she is going to retire. She'll
probably run that children's library until she dies.

The unfortunate reality is that you will have to try another
strategy. One approach that she might relate to is a story. That's
right, call Miss Prosch into your office and tell her a story about all

the bad children's librarians that you have banished to the library dumpster when they begin scaring young children. That's a form of motivation that she can obviously relate to. So that you won't seem too cruel, tell her that you've just had wall to wall carpeting installed down there.

I'm sure that this will cause her to re-evaluate her story time discipline program. It's a message she won't be able to misinterpret.

Regards,
Will

When You Lose a Library Van, You Save on Gas and Oil

Dear Will,

I am a division head in a large state library agency, and one of my biggest responsibilities is keeping track of our rather large fleet of motorized vehicles – cars, bookmobiles, minivans, and delivery trucks. In total we have 57 different vehicles.

As part of my yearly budget preparation process, each December I try to make an attempt at doing an inventory of my fleet to check the age, condition, and mileage of each vehicle. This inventory is difficult because so much of my rolling stock is constantly out on the road.

This year I discovered that one of my vans is not only missing but has been missing (as far as I can tell from my rather spotty records) for at least three years. This situation goes beyond embarrassment and moves into the realm of humiliation. Think about it – I have misplaced a $15,000 van. This will not greatly enhance my job security let alone lead me further down my career development track.

Now here's my dilemma: If I do the right thing and report that the van is missing there is a good chance that I will be fired. That will mean, in essence, that my library career will be over. I mean, what am I going to put in the blank on the application form under the question, "Why did you leave your last job?" – that I got canned for losing a $15,000 delivery van? I'm 53 years old and the only thing I'm qualified to do besides library work is sell microwave ovens at J.C. Penney's.

This leads me to option number two – ignore the missing van. It's been missing for three years without anyone, from the governor on down to the lowliest janitor, having the faintest clue that it is missing. Why should I be overly conscientious, therefore, and report this loss at the risk of losing my livelihood?

My state is a large state, and the state government is an enormous bureaucracy of which I am but one small piece of seaweed. Do you know how much my state spent on toilet paper alone last year? Over $2,000,000. So why should I have to report the loss of a mere $15,000 van?

Sincerely,
RED

Dear Red,

Your correlation between the toilet paper and the missing library van, although impressive, does not obscure the fact that you have lost a van. Think of that. You have lost a van.

Although the van itself is a problem, it is really symptomatic of a larger problem. You are an incompetent administrator.

Vans are not casually lost like a set of car keys. You don't simply misplace a van. It's not the kind of a thing that you look under the sofa for. A van is very hard to lose – even in a big bureaucracy.

But what's even worse than losing a van is losing a van and not even noticing that it is missing for three years. That takes talent.

You really only have one option – report the missing van to your supervisor. Sure, you're not going to win the employee of the month award but if you play your cards right you won't get fired either.

My experience is that large state bureaucracies are very forgiving. In short, I don't think anyone will be that upset about your losing the van. The key for you is how you present the matter to your supervisor.

I suggest a good news/bad news approach. Tell him that the good news is that for three years you have saved the state a significant amount of money on gasoline and oil. Then tell him that the bad news is that this savings is the result of losing a delivery van.

Come to think of it, if your state government is anything like mine, you probably will win the employee of the month award.

All the Best,
Will

The Librarian Who Has Eggs Benedict for Breakfast Is Not to Be Taken Lightly

Dear Will,

Last week I attended the annual conference of the American Library Association and had a horrid experience that I just cannot get out of my mind.

First of all let me say that I was in a hurry. Why the members of the Social Responsibilities Round Table persist in having meetings at eight o'clock in the morning is beyond me. It's almost like they just can't wait to start talking about war, poverty, and the ozone layer. Don't get me wrong, I'd much rather talk about war, poverty, and the ozone layer than added entries and authority files. I just don't like doing it first thing in the morning.

The second thing you should know is that I am a breakfast person. I don't say this out of any sense of moral superiority. It's a simple biological reality with me that if I don't eat breakfast I get this hollow feeling around mid-morning that can only be filled by chocolate, which I should not eat because of my acne and soft teeth.

It turns out that as an occupational group we librarians are very breakfast oriented. "We serve more breakfasts when the librarians are in town than at any other time" is what the maitre d' said as he seated me at a table after I had waited in line for 15 minutes at the hotel coffee shop.

After five more minutes a waitress arrived and I promptly ordered my standard two fried eggs, bacon, toast, and coffee without even bothering to look at the menu. It was 20 minutes to meeting time. Since the Social Responsibilities people expect you to be responsible about time, I punctuated my order by saying to the waitress, "Could you put a rush on it."

This admonition I figured would be about as productive as asking the Pope to do his next mass in rap. It was, therefore, with a great deal of shock that I greeted the platter of food that the waitress plunked down in front of me only two and a half minutes later.

I know that I should have been skeptical but like I said I was hungry and in a hurry. Hungry men don't ask questions when somebody puts food in front of them. The fact is I never enjoyed breakfast as much in my life. Those eggs were a treat. They were poached and placed on a kind of open sandwich of English muffin and Canadian bacon topped with a thick, rich, creamy sauce.

"What a nice thing to do to eggs," is what I told the waitress as she refilled my coffee cup. She gave me one of those smiles that you give crazy people and handed me the bill which came to $17.95. "SEVENTEEN DOLLARS AND NINETY-FIVE CENTS!" I screamed at her. "HOW COULD EGGS COST SEVENTEEN DOLLARS AND NINETY-FIVE CENTS?"

"Not eggs," she said, "eggs Benedict."

Now, Will, I am not a sophisticated man – I admit that. I have heard the term "eggs Benedict" just as I have heard the term "oysters Rockefeller" and I know they both sound very expensive but I had no idea that what I was eating that morning was eggs Benedict. It struck me as very unfair, therefore, that I should have to pay the price for eggs Benedict.

Unfortunately, neither the waitress, the maitre d', or the hotel manager saw it that way. I was stuck with the $17.95 bill which really put a crimp on the rest of my conference since my city only pays a per diem food allowance of $20.

I ask you, was it socially responsible of the hotel to take advantage of my ignorance of eggs Benedict in such greedy way?

Sincerely,

STILL BENT OUT OF SHAPE

Dear Bent,

Such ethical issues are beyond my modest abilities. You might take the issue up with a moral theologian. All I can offer is the old cliché that "Ignorance of the law is no excuse."

But look at the sunny side of your egg experience:

(A) You've had you cultural horizons widened. You now know the rather considerable pleasures of eating eggs Benedict.

(B) You got lightning fast service and weren't late for your Social Responsibilities Round Table meeting.

(C) Some poor sap (hopefully a rich lawyer) who was looking forward to the considerable pleasures of eating eggs Benedict got stuck with your fried eggs.

(D) The cholesterol level of eggs Benedict is surely significantly lower than that of bacon and fried eggs.

(E) Your standing in the profession probably went up immeasur-

ably. I'm sure word spread quickly through the conference that you
are a man of considerable distinction. Librarians who are daring
enough to splurge on eggs Benedict for breakfast in a crowded coffee
shop are never taken lightly.

Regards,
Will

When It Comes to Children, Bondage Is Always Preferable to Anarchy

Dear Will,

Have you noticed the phenomenon of children being chained to
their mothers? Admittedly "chained" may be overstating it a bit, but
these kids definitely are being leashed. Right in our library I've seen
as many as three kids yoked together at one time to their mother
with one of those plastic leashes that looks like a telephone cord. I
am completely appalled by small children being treated as domestic
animals.

Actually it's not just in the library that you see this abuse. It's
everywhere – at church, in fast food restaurants, and all over the
mall. Do you agree with me that this is a rather cruel way to treat
children and what do you think we can do to prevent it from happening in our libraries?

Sincerely,
CONCERNED ABOUT LEGAL FORMS OF CHILD ABUSE

Dear Concerned,

Yes, I have noticed the trend toward child leashing. Twenty
years ago I would have found the practice to be appalling but today I
welcome it.

Perhaps I am getting older and my tolerance for children is
diminishing, although in truth I have always felt that infancy and
toddlerhood are two of God's worst miscalculations. How much more

pleasant the whole concept of parenthood would be without the dirty diapers, the incessant wailing, the frustrations of colic, and the absolute torture of trying to communicate with human beings who cannot verbalize their most basic thoughts. Starting a family would be a much more palatable proposition if children came out of the womb ready to dribble a basketball or paint a watercolor.

The measure of a civilization can in large part be taken on the basis of how adults care for their young. Our society, unfortunately, has tilted toward a posture of neglect. How much easier it is to let children play out their unruliest whims than to make even the feeblest attempt at discipline.

As so often happens when the social pendulum swings toward anarchy there occurs a backlash to the other extreme. In this case the option of bondage is actively exercised.

Leashing is simply the other side of the same coin of child neglect. It is much easier to tie a child down than to expend the effort to inculcate a respect for social responsibility and civilized behavior.

Despite its obvious cruelty, leashing is an option that is preferable to letting children disturb whatever social order we have left. At least a chained child is not a safety threat to himself or to others.

Regards,
Will

A Good Cry Is Worth a Thousand Words

Dear Will,

For four years I wanted to be a library director. Every time a director's job was advertised in *L.J.* I applied for it. It didn't matter if it was for New York Public or New Onion Public. I applied. I was desperate—desperate enough to send out over 350 résumés. In each and every case I was rejected.

Some of my rejections were nicer than others. Frequently I never even got the courtesy of a rejection notice. It was as if they

thought my application was some kind of a joke that was not meant to be taken seriously. Sometimes I would receive a form letter, but rarely would it have any trace of the milk of human kindness. If the form of my rejections varied, the reason for them never did – I had no director experience.

At times I got discouraged, but I never gave up. It always occurred to me that I might get lucky. The president of the board of the library where I was applying might be a graduate of my college or a friend of my father's. Or perhaps the search committee might be attracted to the bold first statement of my letter of introduction – "If you feel you're ready for an innovative library director who thinks that there should be subject headings for fiction, then I'm your guy!"

What finally ended the futility of my job search was the quite unexpected death of my own director. At 48 she was not what you would call an older woman, nor did she appear to be particularly unhealthy. To my knowledge she was not a drinker or a smoker and she most assuredly did not engage in unsafe sex. In fact she probably never engaged in safe sex either.

She died at her desk. That I suppose is not unusual. Untold hundreds of executives have literally worked themselves to death. It's one of those occupational hazards that apparently can't be avoided.

What was unusual about this situation was that Miss Ogelsby's death went, according to the coroner, undiscovered for two, possibly two and a half, days. Before you draw any errant conclusions that I and my ambitious career goals were somehow responsible for Miss O's demise, please know that the coroner was quick to add that her death was as sudden and natural as an earthquake. She suffered a massive "all hell's breaking loose" coronary and was dead in a matter of seconds. "Her arteries were as hard as PVC pipe filled with concrete," is what the coroner said.

All the same he was somewhat puzzled by the length of time it took us to discover her cold and rigid body. "Didn't anyone notice that things were a bit awry?" he asked with more amazement than suspicion. Cindy from circulation was quick to explain. "Not really. Miss O. often spent hours, days actually, in her office with the door closed. She did not enjoy being interrupted. We were not to disturb her until she opened her door and emerged. Sometimes she would emerge as often as two, three, or even four times a day. At other times there were entire weeks when we only caught a glimpse of her coming and going. How were we to know that she was dead?"

That of course was why I was so anxious to become a director. Miss O. could shut out the world while I, a lowly reference librarian, had to endure an endless parade of patrons who had an uncanny propensity to ask inane questions. Quite frankly, I had grown tired of the public by my second or third year on the job.

While daydreaming I would plot ways to murder the next fat person who wanted to know where the books on weight control were. I can't tell you how desperate I was to be finished with the humility of helping people evaluate the relative merits of liposuction and stomach staples. The director's office was the only hope I had for professional survival. Once there I could shut out the public, work with my staff, and read Proust to my heart's content. But my 350 rejections had all but taken away any such hopes.

And then of course Miss Ogelsby's left ventricle ripped rather dramatically from her aorta and three days later (one day after the corpse had been discovered), Mr. Salter, the president of the board, came up to me while I was sitting at the reference desk and said, "Do you think you could keep an eye on things around here now that Miss Ogelsby has left?"

You'd think from the tone of his voice that Miss O. had simply departed for a three week Caribbean cruise. That was two years ago and nothing else was ever said to me about officially becoming director. My salary was increased and I was instructed to move into Miss Ogelsby's office, but there was never any official announcement of my appointment. It was almost as if Ogelsby's Caribbean cruise turned into a long term sabbatical. I fully expect to come in some morning and find her seated at my desk.

And the truth is I wouldn't mind having that happen because I am sick and tired of playing counselor, psychologist, and cheerleader to my staff. I suppose I brought it on myself. Shortly after Miss O. died I got everybody together and said that I wanted to create an atmosphere of open communication and that I would always make myself available to anyone who had a problem.

That is obviously what opened the floodgates of tears. Not a week goes by that someone doesn't come into my office for a good cry. I myself am not a crier, and I don't admire the trait in others. To me crying is manipulation, nothing more and nothing less. I'm almost positive that my employees think they can get what they want from me by crying. They figure that I'll feel terribly sympathetic or terribly embarrassed, and they're absolutely right. I give them what they want just to get them out of my office. I'd rather have them yell at me than cry.

The problem is I just can't take this anymore. I don't have the emotional hardness to be an administrator. I'm spending a fortune on Kleenex and I have secretly started drinking on my lunch break. If I had wanted to be a counselor I would have majored in psychology. I wish I could mastermind a strategic retreat back to the reference desk. As it is I'm hiding in my office (shades of Miss Ogelsby) with the door locked most of the time.

Help!

Sincerely,

A DRY EYE IN A WET WORLD

Dear Dry,

First you hate your patrons and then you hate your staff. It sounds on the surface like you have a real problem dealing with people and that you should give serious consideration to finding a job as a full time hermit.

Actually this may shock you but you really aren't a misanthrope; you just think you are. The fact that your patrons were willing to share their very personal weight problems with you and that your employees are lining up to cry in your office are pretty good indications that you do have definite potential to become a genuine "people person."

The evidence strongly suggests that your staff likes you, trusts you, and feels very secure in your presence. When two people get together and strong emotions (crying, yelling, and throwing things) result, that is a definite sign that real communication is taking place.

Think about it – you only express strong emotions in front of someone whom you trust. We tend to cry in front of our friends, not our enemies. For instance, I would never cry in front of someone whom I thought would ridicule or berate me for my tears.

Ninety percent of what we communicate to others is nonverbal, and crying is one of the most eloquent forms of nonverbal communication. So don't feel put upon; feel flattered.

And by the way, you should allow yourself the luxury of a good cry from time to time. There's nothing like it to purge your heart and soul of all frustrations. It's almost as good as throwing plates!

Regards,
Will

Give Clark Kent a Break – Put Your Pay Phone in the Restroom

Dear Will,

In designing the floor plan for a new library what do you think is the best location for a pay phone?

I have searched the literature on library architecture and have found wonderful advice on stack layouts, circulation desk designs, lighting levels, and even storage space, but I can find no mention of pay phones.

What is your view on this subject?

Sincerely,
DOUG

Dear Doug,

Good question! The first thing you will find is that unfortunately the self contained phone booth is a relic of the past. It has been quietly but systematically replaced by simple open-air phone pedestals which offer no real privacy. One wonders where the Clark Kent of the '90s will change into his Superman suit.

Besides being a makeshift dressing room, the old fashioned phone booth had its advantages. First, it provided a private and relatively quiet space in which to carry on a conversation and second it provided college fraternities and sororities an opportunity to challenge the world record for phone booth stuffing.

But phone booths, for all their conveniences, also had their downsides. Increasingly during the 1970s and '80s they became places of terror. An alarming number of rapes, muggings, slashings, and even homicides took place in phone booths. Once in a booth, a phone caller was trapped and at the mercy of an assailant. The disappearance of the phone booth naturally makes the placing of a pay phone in the library rather problematic. Libraries of all types are rather public, and it is therefore difficult to pinpoint locations in library buildings where the privacy of the phone caller can be assured without disturbing the peace of library users.

My solution is to put pay phones in the restrooms. Restrooms, after all, are reserved for our most private functions. They are therefore perfectly suited for pay phones. You can talk to your heart's content in a restroom and not have to worry about disturbing anyone who is trying to read a book unless, of course, that person is using the toilet stall as a study carrel.

Sometimes life's most vexing questions have the simplest of solutions. The location of the library pay phone is a good case in point.

Sincerely,
Will

A Gravy Train Sandwich Is Not Without Nutritional Value

Dear Will,

According to my co-worker, Harry, librarians need to work harder at "radiating the joy of living." He thinks that we are a profession of dullards and sourpusses.

Unfortunately it appears that Harry has taken it upon himself to rectify the profession's image problem all by himself – at my expense. Why he's picking on me I don't know. Some people say he loves me, and other people say he hates me. I didn't mind him tampering with my circulation records (everybody knows that I couldn't possibly have 319 overdue books), and I didn't mind him putting a fake dismissal notice in my mailbox (everybody knows that I am the best foreign language cataloger on staff and that the library couldn't function without me), and I didn't mind him streaking naked past me in the parking lot at night (Harry's body, after all, is quite ridiculous).

But I do get upset when he purloins my peanut butter sandwich and replaces it with one filled with essence of Gravy Train. This goes beyond practical joking into the realm of harassment.

I brought the matter up to our head of human resources, but he simply smiled condescendingly at me and said, "Lighten up." This attitude infuriates me.

How can I put an end to Harry's puerile shenanigans?

Sincerely,
NOT WILD ABOUT HARRY

Dear Not,

Lighten up!

Harry has officially gotten your goat. The angrier you get at his antics, the more he will continue to victimize you. He smells blood. He picked you because you obviously are an easy target. Your sense of humor does not appear to be your dominant trait.

If I were you I'd expect some weird phone calls, some strange things added to your morning coffee, some additional computer mischief, and some things missing from your desk. My advice is to get a burglar-proof lunchbox and change the locks on your doors. The Gravy Train sandwich is bad, but not that bad. It could have been Kitty Litter. Gravy Train is much more preferable to Kitty Litter. It has considerable nutritional value while Kitty Litter has none.

If you want to put an end to all of Harry's nonsense I'd suggest beating him at his own game. In short, you need to fight back. Start by doing something to his car. Most men treasure their cars above all else. Siphon the gas out of his gas tank, pour honey on his roof and hood, and stick Coke in his windshield washer container.

Then when he gets incensed, step back and tell him to "lighten up." I guarantee the practical jokes will stop and you can go back to being a sourpuss.

Regards,
Will

You Can Rip Someone's Lungs Out and Still Be Supportive

Dear Will,

I am a director of a fairly large public library and I try to fit the role of the modern manager in that I believe in participative management, facilitative supervision, and supportive leadership.

My employees are more than mere parts of a large, impersonal organizational machine. To me they are family, and my door is always open to them for whatever they need. My experience is that if you treat your employees with understanding, they will treat you with understanding.

For instance, if someone on staff is not performing well on the job I try to be holistic about it. Is the employee having a job related problem or is there something wrong at home? That's the question that I want to answer because unhappy people make nonproductive workers. My job, therefore, is to alleviate the source of unhappiness. Sometimes I can do this with a change in working conditions and sometimes I can do it with some simple heartfelt advice. At all times, however, I try to stay strictly nonjudgmental.

This benign philosophy of mine, however, is being stretched to the limit with my secretary, Cecilia. Cecilia has always been loyal, dependable, discreet, and productive – in short, the perfect secretary. But last month everything changed when her husband left her for a much younger woman. That's when it seemed like I went from being a library director to a shrink.

At first, Cecilia went through major ego problems. Every morning she would come into my office and ask me if I found her attractive

and every day I would have to say, "Cecilia I find you absolutely stunning!" But after a few mornings that wasn't good enough. Cecilia wanted me to go into specifics. She wanted me to pinpoint exactly what I found so stunning about her. Besides being embarrassing, this form of therapy became time consuming because if I said, "Cecilia, you have great legs," she would ask, "What about my eyes, don't you like my eyes?" It got so I had to mention something specific about every aspect of her anatomy. ("Cecilia, you have the most sensuous pancreas. It no doubt is one of your most intense erogenous zones. If I weren't married I'd just love to give your pancreas a deep massage.")

After we both tired of Biology 101, we got into the whole area of divorce law and high finance, two subjects that I have absolutely no expertise in. But that didn't stop Cecilia. She would ask me every question imaginable about child custody, community property, and liquidation of assets, and I would end up saying something ridiculous like, "No, Cecilia, if I were you I wouldn't invest in corporate junk bonds just right now." The truth is I don't even know what a corporate junk bond is but it doesn't sound very profitable to me.

Now she is into hatred – ugly, backbiting hatred. Although as part of the divorce settlement, she is supposed to let Harold have the tent trailer, she has decided to play hardball and not give it up. Now all I ever hear anymore around the office are the words "tent trailer." The whole staff is getting involved. You go to the staff lounge for coffee and all people talk about is the Great Tent Trailer War.

Frankly I've had it. Against my very nature I am feeling very nonparticipative, nonfacilitative, and nonsupportive. I want to call Cecilia into my office and tell her that if I ever hear the words "tent trailer" again I will rip her lungs out.

I feel terribly guilty about these negative feelings of mine, but it's getting to the point that I don't feel I can control my anger anymore. What should I do?

Sincerely,

JACK

Dear Jack,

Remember that time that Phil Donahue got into a fist fight at the airport? In my opinion it did him a world of good.

What you need to do is call Cecilia into your office and tell her that if you ever hear the words "tent trailer" again that you will rip her lungs out. Do not feel guilty about this. It is a perfectly legitimate thing to do and even has a name – Reality Therapy.

More than anything Cecilia needs some reality. You'll be doing her a big favor.

Regards,

Will

Desk Envy Is an Early Sign of Neurosis and Should Be Treated Immediately

Dear Will,

I am a new director in a fairly large public library (staff of 100), and shortly after my appointment, I undertook, with full board approval, a massive reorganization of the staff which involved setting new priorities, writing new job descriptions, creating new job titles, and transferring people from one department to another. As a result, a number of people had to change offices and work stations.

To minimize staff resistance I made it clear that no one would be fired, demoted, or have to take a cut in pay. Despite those reassurances, I still braced myself for the inevitable back-biting and infighting that normally occurs when you make changes in the daily

work routine of your employees. But what I didn't expect was the Great Overhang Controversy.

The Great Overhang Controversy occurred when I moved Sheila, my deputy director for technical services, out of the administrative wing and into the technical services room. I did this because I felt it was more important for her to be near her employees than to be near me. When it comes to tech services I am very hands off. I told Sheila she should look at the move as a compliment since it was a sign of my utmost trust and confidence in her. I didn't need to be looking over her shoulder.

Grudgingly Sheila moved into her new office, which I understand is seven square inches larger than Sheila's old office. The rumor around the library is that Sheila got down on her hands and knees and took the measurements herself. I don't know what we would have done if the new office had been seven square inches smaller.

The trouble didn't start until after Bill moved into Sheila's old office. Bill, you see, is a newly minted M.L.S. holder with an undergraduate degree in accounting. I felt his skills were being wasted in the periodicals room, and I moved him upstairs to the ad-ministrative wing to serve as my administrative assistant and to coordinate the library's $5,000,000 budget. Although Bill is making the same salary in administration that he was making in periodicals, Sheila obviously resents his quick rise to her old office.

That's why she has made such a big deal out of the "overhang" issue. She complains that the overhang on Bill's desk is six inches wider than the overhang on her desk. Sheila believes that the size of a person's desk is an indication of that person's importance in the organization, and she believes strongly that she is more important than Bill.

The bottom line is that she has demanded her old desk back. Bill doesn't care. It would be easy for me to give her Bill's desk but what bothers me is that I don't want to cater to her childishness.

What do you advise?

Sincerely,
KATHERINE

*   *   *

Dear Katherine,

If you give in to her demands, you might as well resign right now. It is true that the psychological needs of today's employees require more than a good paycheck. People do need to feel appreciated and wanted, but Sheila's ego problems about desk size border on the abnormal.

Don't give her Bill's desk; give her a certificate for six free counseling sessions instead.

Sincerely,
Will

Look Closely at Your Lover's Toes Before You Gaze Deeply into Her Eyes

Dear Will,

I never thought something like this would happen to me. I am a cataloger (specializing in Festschriften) in a large private research library. I used to love routine. Nirvana for me was getting on a roll and doing the same thing day after day after day. Consistency and predictability were my gods. I considered good habits to be the tools of the successful man.

Everyday I would get up at six, jog (always 2.3 miles), shower, eat breakfast (always Cheerios sprinkled with wheat germ), get dressed (always a red tie, gray slacks, and a white Oxford shirt), go to work, catalog, eat lunch (always seven ounces of carrot sticks and celery stalks), go back to work, catalog, stop at Sincerity on the way home for one martini (always on the rocks with a twist of lemon), go home, cook dinner (either chicken or fish), watch Brokaw, read Trollope, watch Carson's monologue, shower, brush, floss, and go to bed.

Hey, don't laugh. It worked for me – day after day after day. Reality may be hell and life may be suffering, but I was alive. I was

fit. I was productive. I was not like all the other people in America suffering from lawsuits, divorces, and stomach gas.

Then a month ago I made the mistake of interrupting my routine. I went to the A.L.A. annual conference in Chicago and fell desperately in love with a cataloger named Kim. Her specialty was ephemera. She was waiting in line at the hotel coffee shop for lunch right behind me. The place was so congested that the maitre d' suggested that to expedite things we should sit together at a table for two. At first I resisted but when I looked into her eyes I was hooked.

Ordinarily I would scoff at a concept so amorphous as animal magnetism, but call it what you want, the fact is a strong and riveting bond developed instantly between the two of us. I couldn't take my eyes off her, and she was lost in space with me. I haven't the slightest idea what I had for lunch that day. When it came time to go back to the conference we decided to take off our shoes instead and walk barefoot through the little park across the street from the Convention Center.

For four hours we told each other the stories of our lives and discovered that we both had the same motivation for getting into cataloging – to tidy up the world a bit. I should have noticed at the time that her feet were rather hairy but I was riveted on her eyes.

We went back to our respective rooms to get changed for an evening of drinks, dinner, and dancing. As the evening wore on our instant attraction deepened into something more profound. We discovered that we were both passionate about Albert Brooks, Maynard Ferguson (the early Maynard Ferguson), Andy Warhol (the later Andy Warhol), Sergio Leone, the Broadway production of *Cats*, the use of semicolons rather than commas in creating bibliographic records, and taco salads.

We also discovered that we were passionate about each other – not only metaphysically but physically. Despite our mixed sense of spiritual exhilaration and raw passion we agreed that it was premature for us to consummate our carnal desires.

"Let's not let our lust interfere with our love," is the way she so elegantly articulated the almost transcendental nature of our attraction. We would not let the earthiness of a brief sexual encounter

muddy the extraordinary connection of thoughts, feelings, and emotions that we had made.

The next day it was more of the same. If there was still a library
conference going on we certainly didn't notice it. We gazed into each
other's eyes and talked about country houses in Cornwall, seascapes
in Nova Scotia, sagebrush in New Mexico, and sunsets over the Indian Ocean. At midnight we departed, she to her room and me to
mine.

But I could not sleep so I called her. "I have," she said, "a bottle
of Chardonnay. Let's pour some for each other and look for rainbows
in our wineglasses." We barely had three sips when I began to gently
but seductively undress her. Believe me I didn't want to have sex
with her; I just wanted to make love – wonderful, angelic love. With
my gentle fingers I probed and explored the landscape of her body.
The stubs of hair that I felt on her chest greatly disturbed me but I
was absolutely horrified when I felt the presence of a male organ.
My true love was a man! This Kim was a he! "Don't let this stand
between us," was the last thing Kim ever said to me.

The conference is over, and I am back in my routine – my sweet
routine.

Sincerely,
TEMPORARILY BLINDED BY LOVE

Dear Blinded,

I'm not sure what to say. As far as love stories go, yours is the
most unique I've ever read. Actually it is also fairly relevant to the
times. I understand that transvestitism is now more in vogue than
ever, which I suppose means that you should always look closely at
your lover's toes before you gaze deeply into her eyes.

Thanks for sharing your pain so that others may learn from your
mistakes.

Regards,
Will

*   *   *

Don't Judge the Homeless Until You've Slept Over a Grate

Dear Will,

Few institutions are as confronted by the homeless problem as the public library. Our public library is a good example. It is located in a large metropolitan area in the Sunbelt, and in the winter months it attracts a diverse array of homeless people – young and old, male and female.

Back in the '50s when I got started in public library work these types of people were simply regarded as bums. At that time they were seen as an unavoidable fact of life. They were neither objects of sympathy nor victims of derision. They were as much a fixture of American life as potholes, leaky roofs, and automobile accidents.

It was generally felt that "bums" were nonconformists who had made a conscious decision to live a carefree life on the road. It was their choice and their choice alone to detach themselves from the trials and tribulations of holding a job, raising a family, and owning a home. While some bums may have chosen their peripatetic lifestyle as a permanent vocational calling, others were simply hitchhiking or riding the rails to satisfy a youthful and temporary wanderlust. This second variety of bum came to be romanticized in the works of Jack Kerouac.

Today, however, the term bum is as déclassé as the terms "colored" and "retarded," and in a way I am sorry to see the term go. I mean who in their right mind would pick up a Kerouac novel entitled *The Dharma Homeless?*

Actually my policy in dealing with the homeless today is the same policy that I used 30 years ago to deal with bums. I expect everyone who uses my library – and that includes the homeless – to be orderly, fully dressed, and reasonably bathed.

The reasonably bathed criterion is the one that has my younger librarians upset. They think that besides being impossible to define, it discriminates against those who have neither the means nor the opportunity to shower and wash on a periodical basis. My response is that extreme body odor (irrespective of its social causes or economic

origin) is as intolerable as other forms of inappropriate library
behavior such as fighting, loud talking, or brandishing a handgun. If
egregious body odor drives responsible patrons out of the reading
room, then it is the responsibility of the director to kick out the
offender.

This policy, however, does not sit well with the new breed of
librarian who sees it as our professional duty to understand and call
attention to the plight of the homeless. I say let the homeless get
jobs. (There happens to be a McDonald's down the street from the
library that has three job openings right now!) Are we social workers
or are we librarians? If we are too soft on the homeless, word will
spread and we will be inundated with even more of them.

One of my young reference librarians is so upset with my attitude that he has challenged me to go homeless for a week and then come back to the library and make policy. How outrageous!

Sincerely,
BOB, A TRADITIONAL LIBRARIAN

Dear Bob,

Isn't it unfortunate, Bob, that the weather gets so warm in your Sunbelt haven that it attracts the urban unfortunates of the North. Your attitude toward the homeless reflects a certain unwillingness to accept the fact that something is rather rotten in America today.

How thoughtless of the homeless to invade your city of Rustbelt refugees. Just when your citizens thought they had escaped the homeless of Newark, Cleveland, and Detroit, they show up on your doorstep looking for spare change and sympathy. How inconsiderate!

But this doesn't seem to bother you one iota, Bob. You won't be moved by their plight. You'll take a hard line. They chose their lifestyle, now let them live it. It is their decided preference to stink.

Bob, ordinarily I'd say that social experiments like the one suggested by your reference librarian are unnecessary. After all, do we have to serve in the frontlines in order to experience the horrors of war? But in your case I would prescribe not one but two weeks with the homeless. I'm confident that two weeks in their heart of darkness will obliterate the word "bums" from your vocabulary forever.

Regards,
Will

If You Don't Like the Word "Librarian" Get Out of the Profession

Dear Will,

As head of adult services for a medium sized public library, I have administrative responsibility for six reference librarians, two

audiovisual librarians, one adult programs librarian, and one acquisitions librarian. Overall, they're a great group of people to work with.

Each year as part of my organizational spring cleaning program, I allow these ten librarians the time and money to get together for a one day retreat at a location of their choice. Usually they select a conference room at a local hotel where they can enjoy some privacy away from the hustle and bustle of the library.

While they are gone, the library director, the head of the children's department, the head of tech services, and I staff their desks in the library. It's a win-win situation. The librarians get a chance to get away from phones and patrons to talk, think, argue, reflect, and complain amongst themselves, and we administrators get a chance to see firsthand what their jobs are really like.

The only thing that I require of the librarians is that they come back from the retreat with a series of recommendations for changes that they would like to see happen in the working conditions and organizational climate of the library. They do have one limitation—their changes should not cost an arm and a leg.

Each year I tell them that anyone can create a wish list with unlimited funding but that it takes real creativity to make changes with an empty wallet. This year, I must say, they finally listened. Their main recommendation was indeed very inexpensive. All they wanted were new job titles. They told me that this wouldn't cost me a penny.

Naturally I was delighted with their sense of fiscal responsibility. But this immediately cooled when they handed me the list of new titles. The reference librarians want to be "User Services Coordinators"; the audiovisual librarians want to be "Multi-Media Specialists"; the adult programs librarian wants to be a "Community Cultural Programs Manager"; and the acquisitions librarian wants to be a "Resource Management Analyst."

Do you think that the employees want these new titles because they sound more impressive than their old ones, and that some day they think they can parlay these fancy titles into a higher salary? I have no problem with giving them these titles now, but will it cost me later? I mean a "User Services Coordinator" does sound more high powered than a "reference librarian" and a "Resource Management Analyst" does sound pricier than an "acquisitions librarian."

I want to please the staff, but I am skeptical of their true intentions.

Sincerely,
DON'T KNOW WHAT TO DO

Dear Don't Know,

Besides the obvious objection that the new job titles reek with bureaucratese and mean absolutely nothing to the average person, I have a real problem with the fact that the words "librarian" and "library" do not appear once in any of them.

I am one of those old-fashioned people who happens to think that the word "librarian" is special. Throughout history librarians have been largely responsible for saving and preserving the literary treasures of Western Civilization. It is a noble calling to be a "librarian" just as it is a noble calling to be a doctor or a priest.

But it is not a noble calling to be a "User Services Coordinator," a "Health Services Analyst," or a "Spiritual Services Specialist." In fact, those are the kinds of generic and ambiguous sounding job titles that city managers and city councils love to cut in the midst of a budget crunch.

For your library's good and the good of your staff, don't let your librarians become soulless bureaucrats. A librarian is worthy of the taxpayers' dollars; a "Resource Management Analyst" is not.

Sincerely,
Will

*   *   *

For Peace of Mind Establish Your Interface with NECRONET Today

Dear Will,

    I am one of those people who does not like surprises. As a result I am something of a planner and a worrier. Especially on trips. I plan everything and worry about everything. The airplane will be overbooked, the airplane will crash, the hotel will be overbooked, my reservations will be lost, I'll eat out and get food poisoning, I'll get pickpocketed, I'll lose my Visa card, I won't remember my medical insurance number, I'll get a ride with a homicidal cab driver, the rental car agency will be overbooked, I'll crack up my rental car, or I'll get lost and run out of gas. These are only some of my concerns. For this reason I like to stay home and watch H.B.O. on my vacations. I like routine and familiarity. Don't volunteer me for any trips on the Space Shuttle.

    About the only place I go anymore is to A.L.A. conferences, and I pretty much have to go there because I am a member of the S.C.C.T.F. – the Serbo-Croation Catalogers' Task Force. There aren't many of us around. Next year I could be the vice-chair. What I like about A.L.A. conventions is that you can schedule your entire conference right down to the minute several months in advance because A.L.A. is so good about getting their program brochures out in the mail well in advance of the actual conference.

    My question for you, however, is not about A.L.A. conferences. My real concern is with the ultimate trip that we will all have to make sooner or later to the hereafter. I am not scared to die and I really don't have any objections to the concept of death. After all, who wants to live forever – there are only so many times that you can take out the garbage. But I just hate the uncertainty of it all.

    What will heaven be like? Are there libraries in heaven? Please say yes because I'm not sure I'd even want to go if there are no libraries. I'm not the type of person who would adjust well to a post-life career change. Serbo-Croatian cataloging is my one and only love.

Sincerely,

J.C. (JUST CURIOUS)

Dear J.C.,

First of all don't believe the professional religious types. Their version of the celestial paradise is so unappealing (personally I hate harps and I'm not real big on clouds either) that it makes God look like an almighty nerd. Since God is not a nerd (burning bushes are not the mark of a nerd) that version of heaven simply does not exist.

So don't worry yourself that you're going to be spending eternity employed as a harpist or a cloud gondolier.

What is heaven like? Simple. All you have to do is take a close look at the Gospel according to John which starts out with "In the beginning was the Word." Now you may ask what is "the Word"? Conveniently St. John answers that question. He says that "the Word was with God and that God was the Word." That's pretty fascinating. God, if He can be defined at all, obviously has something to do with words, language, and wisdom. It sounds to me that if we are to take the Gospel according to John seriously, then we have to conclude that heaven is probably a place of learning and enlightenment. Logically, libraries would assume a very important function there. So stop worrying. I'm sure that there is as big a shortage of Serbo-Croatian catalogers in heaven as there is on earth. You won't need to make a career change.

Finally, there is a library network – NECRONET – that you should know about. NECRONET's motto is "We are dying to serve." It is made up of deceased librarians. There are apparently three or four psychics in the California Library Association who have established an interface with the members of NECRONET. They basically corroborate the picture of heaven that I have described for you. I also understand that A.L.A. will soon be offering eternal memberships to NECRONET at the special price of $139.95.

Yours,
Will

The Problem with Natural Plants Is That They Always Die; the Problem with Fake Plants Is That They Never Die

Dear Will,

Last month we opened a large new main library. Although I had spent literally thousands of hours planning the library and studying blueprints, there were some things that surprised me about the building, namely that it was so cavernous. My trustees apparently had the same reaction. A common remark that they made about the building when it was completed was, "It's so big, but it seems so empty and sterile."

Naturally a task force was formed to study the emptiness problem. After considering various ways to re-configure the furniture and rearrange some of the bookstacks, everyone agreed that all the building really needed was some greenery.

That's when the fighting started. I have been in the middle of board wars before but nothing like this. This made the dispute over whether to have red meat at the annual board dinner look like a fairy tale.

On one side of the fight were the natural plant people and on the other side were the silk plant advocates. If you've ever seen the "right-to-life" and "pro choice" people go at it, then you have a good idea about how hot and heavy this controversy has become.

Right now the board is deadlocked 3 to 3 (Elmer Jordan is in the hospital recouperating from heart surgery) and the controversy will continue to fester until Elmer gets out of the hospital and gets back on his feet. Neither side will give an inch. Basically, the natural plant faction hates artificiality and the silk plant side does not want to commit the money to the maintenance that natural plants demand.

Do you have any ideas about how I could get this stalemate off dead-center?

Sincerely,
IN THE MIDDLE

Dear Middle,

A plague on both their houses! Who needs plants, real or fake? Is it a library that you are opening up or a fern bar? Plants, like animals (including dogs, cats, and goldfish) should stay outside where God put them.

Fake plants are fake. I don't care if we're talking silk or plastic or naugahyde, an artificial plant is philosophically an absurd concept. I mean if you're going to go artificial why don't you just go ahead and decorate your library with fake giraffes? They would be much more striking than philodendrons and would take up more space, which is apparently what your objective is. As an aside, I've never heard of a library with too much space. I think you've made history.

There's also a practical problem with fake plants. They are magnets for dust. There is nothing more depressing in this world than a dusty fake plant. So if you plan to put in fake plants you'd better plan on assigning someone on staff to be your artificial plant duster. I'm sure that will be a position of honor for your librarians. Maybe you can rotate the chore.

The other problem with silk plants is that they don't die. Therefore you don't have a good excuse to throw them away when you get tired of looking at them. Dogs die, cats die, and plants die, but fake plants just go on living and living and living. It's horrid to contemplate but do you realize that long after you're gone all the dusty fake plants of the world will still be alive?

On the other hand, the problem with natural plants is that they do die. It's the height of ingratitude. You put all that money into babying your plants and they die on you. But the worst part is that they don't die quickly. They die slowly, first turning yellow and then brown, and all the while that they are dying you are vainly trying to keep them alive. Maybe I'm morbid but when I look at an indoor plant I see a living thing that is in some stage of death.

But I can't in all fairness be completely negative about natural plants because I am convinced that they are one of the reasons why my community has a new main library. Our old building was filled with potted plants, which provided shelter for armies of cockroaches. Over time the building became so infested with these roaches that the idea of a new library began to make more and more sense.

Since the last thing you need is a new building, forget the plants. You might even consider filling all that space with books. I realize that's a bit old fashioned, but I'm sure it would go over big with your patrons.

Regards,
Will

Thank God Mark Twain
Never Lived in Newark

Dear Will,

For years the two biggest controversies to embroil librarians were what I call the "New York–Newark" dispute and the "Mark Twain–Samuel Clemens" debate.

One was a filing issue; the other was a cataloging feud. But now with the advent of computer technology those kinds of petty little professional squabbles have largely become meaningless, and I am sure that no one really misses them. I mean whether you felt "New York" should be filed before "Newark" or whether "Newark" should be filed before "New York" you really couldn't say that it was a life and death issue or even one with the slightest existential or environmental significance.

By in large the Newark–New York controversy was an argument of preference – like trying to decide between Skippy or Peter Pan, and consequently whenever I got drawn into the argument, I felt somehow silly about the amount of passion that I sometimes generated on behalf of Newark. But then you have to understand Newark is where I grew up.

The same goes for the Mark Twain–Samuel Clemens fight. The way we librarians would bare our fangs over that little disagreement you'd think that the very authorship of *Huck Finn* was at stake. You'd think that there were two different men laying claim to having written the book rather than one man who happened to use two different names.

How silly it was for us to expend so much angry rhetoric on such a petty concern. No doubt Mark Twain (or do you prefer Sam Clemens) rolled over in his grave laughing every time we librarians started fighting over his "name." But Mark, wherever you are, I just want you to know that I always came down firmly on the side of "Mark Twain" because I felt you would have wanted it that way in the card catalog.

It occurs to me, however, as I reflect upon the apparent pettiness of our former passions, that those arguments were not just so

much dotting of "i"'s and crossing of "t"'s. They were about something far more important than mere bibliographic niceties. They were really about a rather idealistic notion called uniformity – the idea that you could walk into a library of any type anywhere and find "New York" filed before "Newark" and *Huckleberry Finn* cataloged under "Mark Twain."

What an ambitious undertaking! And just think – it was largely accomplished by the quiet heroes who served so valiantly on the myriad of committees that shaped our Anglo-American cataloging rules.

And now we are computerized and it doesn't matter whether New York comes before Newark or vice-versa because now all you have to do is type the words into the terminal and the computer does all the thinking for you. Isn't that wonderful?

It's wonderful until you realize that there are now dozens of computer systems available and no two of them operate alike. Now when you walk into a library and confront the catalog you must learn the ground rules of that catalog before you can proceed. We have no uniformity like we did with our old card catalogs, and in my opinion the user is the loser.

Is this progress?

> Sincerely,
> SAM

Dear Sam,

The good old days weren't that terrific. Do you also miss wood stoves, glass milk bottles, and window air conditioners?

I am in favor of anything that lessens the need for committees of people with master's degrees to meet and decide whether New York should be filed before Newark. Enough said.

> Regards,
> Will

*   *   *

Always Remember That the Reference Librarian Who Carries a Power Drill into the Bathroom Could Someday Be You

Dear Will,

I am not entirely an innocent and naive man. We are, I realize, living in a sick society. Our murder rate, our addiction to drugs of all kinds (legal and illegal) and our obsession with pornography are the symptoms of a morally restless and deeply disturbed people. The signs of societal deterioration are all around us.

We are not such a depraved people, however, that when certain social ills come to roost on our very own front porch that we don't recoil in shock and revulsion. Despite all the indignities of living in a sick society we do retain a modicum of decency and dignity.

Last Monday my custodian came to me with the news that a series of rather substantial peepholes (two inch diameters) had been drilled in the toilet stalls of our first floor men's bathroom. I instructed him to fill them up and repair the stalls in a most expeditious manner. If there is anything that we library administrators should guarantee our patrons it is a safe and secure restroom experience.

The presence of peepholes shocked me. I had always preferred to think that our library, ensconced as it is in the middle of an affluent suburban community, was immune to the more profligate elements of society. Obviously when sexual perversity invades such strongholds of middle class normalcy it must be counterattacked very vigorously. My taxpayers would demand nothing less.

A mere two days after my janitor had repaired the toilet partitions, the peepholes reappeared in exactly the same places. Like Moses trying to stem the tide of the Red Sea, our janitor once again got out his toolbox and went to work. But twelve hours later the

peepholes were back and this time there were twice as many. Our
sexual pervert was obviously making a bold statement.

Subsequently an undercover policeman was brought in and in a
matter of twelve hours a man wielding a battery operated power
drill was apprehended right in the middle of his act of defacement.
The offender it turned out was Percy, my government documents
specialist. I was mortified. Percy is the type of person who enjoys
reading *The Federal Register* as a leisure time activity.

As I see it, my options are three. I can (1) fire Percy, (2) fire him
and press criminal charges against him, or (3) give him a leave of
absence and require him to seek counseling. I am greatly torn between a sense of revulsion toward anyone who would resort to
peepholes for recreational pleasure and a sense of compassion
toward a fellow librarian whose nine year old son plays on the same
Little League team as my son. What do you recommend?

Sincerely,
SHOCKED AND DISMAYED

Dear Dismayed,

This is a tough one. Percy is obviously a pervert who, although
he has done nothing violent, has violated the human rights of those
using your restrooms. He is obviously a sick man who is crying out
for help. Anybody who openly carries a power drill into a men's room
wants to get caught. Percy is your colleague and your friend. You
need to help him, not destroy him.

I would, therefore, 1) give him a leave of absence without pay, 2)
get him lined up with a good therapist, and 3) forbid him from ever
stepping in a public bathroom again in his life. But for the grace of
God that could be you with the power drill. Middle class America
seethes with unspoken frustration, bitterness, and angst. If Percy is
a voyeur, Sheila in cataloging might be a nymphomaniac, and Donnie
in periodicals might be an ice-pick murderer. Who knows what set of
circumstances would turn any of us to deviant behavior?

The members of a sick society need understanding, not censure.
Our prisons are filled to the brim and that has done no good.

Regards,
Will

Do Not Rake the Leaves
Blowing Through Your Mind

Dear Will,

This may seem picky to you but one of my reference librarians is driving me up a wall because he seems to be incapable of writing simple declarative sentences. He consistently expresses himself in free verse or is it blank verse – I can never remember the difference. And I'm not just talking about post-'em notes or daily reminders, I'm talking about official memoranda, policy recommendations, statistical reports, bibliographies, and even meeting minutes.

For instance, yesterday it was his turn to take notes at our biweekly reference group meetings. This is what he produced:

    wailing

        flailing

            bureaucratic

            ego-flux

                meeting adjourned

                I AM WHOLLY

As head of reference I was not only confused by this drivel but offended as well. What's worse is that he never signs it with his real name but rather with some cockeyed nom de plume like "Cool Papa," "His Wholiness," "Pope Rex," "Papa," "J. Edgar," and "Fred."

On his yearly evaluation form in the section for employee comments he wrote: strivingfailinglearninggrowingstretchingstop. This he signed "DuncemanIII."

He does not speak in such cryptic tones. Person to person he is very nice, polite, and considerate. He is, in fact, a rather shy young man – one who goes out of his way to make all personal encounters as painless as possible.

I have demanded that he stop the poetry but it continues to appear like the leaves blowing around in my backyard in the middle of winter. Where do these leaves come from? The trees are bare and I raked every single leaf up months ago. This is maddening.

Sincerely,

SANDRA

Dear Sandra,

The rather wistful ending to your letter haunts me. The wonderful image of leaves blowing around your yard leads me to believe that you may be a blocked or frustrated poet yourself.

Your reference librarian bugs you because he has a certain panache that you so desperately covet. You wish that like him you had the chutzpah to unleash the free verse that lives within you, but you are too uptight to let go of your inhibitions.

On the other hand, I may be completely missing the point of your blowing leaves. You may simply be a control freak – the worst kind of boss. These poems confound you not because they are an unconventional mode of communication but because you do not understand them and what you do not understand you can't control – like those leaves blowing around in your backyard. "Where do they come from?" It bothers you that you don't know.

For goodness' sake, woman, enjoy the leaves! You are a librarian and you are scared of poetry. This is like a priest who is unnerved by the thought of a Supreme Being. Poetry is the very stuff of librarianship. It is why we exist. It is the very quality that is lacking in our mechanistic society. We need great gobs of poetry to ward off the spiritual disease from which we suffer. We should all be filling our library shelves with poetry.

We've tried everything, have we not, to solve the problems of the Middle East, to patch the hole in the ozone, to stop acid rain, and to put an end to the awful, senseless destruction of the rain forest. Computers don't work, science doesn't work, and prayers to the weak and pitiful gods that we worship on Wall Street do not work.

Poetry, madam, is precisely what is lacking in our lives – the poetry that connects us to the pulsating beat of life and the mysteries of the cosmos. Crown your poet with many crowns; do not censor him. His meeting minutes eloquently describe every library meeting I have ever been to.

As for you, Sandra, you need to relax. Take some time every night and look at the sunset. Go out and get yourself a massage. But most of all take delight in the leaves that dance merrily in your yard and in your mind.

If that's impossible get out of librarianship and get into information science.

Shalom,
Will

*   *   *

The Care and Feeding of Your Circulation Clerks Is Just as Important as the Maintenance of Your Computerized Circulation System

Dear Will,

I am growing a bit concerned about the mental health and welfare of my circulation staff. Admittedly they have been under a lot of stress this summer (June and July are our busiest months because of our very ambitious summer reading program for children), but don't you think it is rather alarming for them to be talking about replacing fines with grotesque forms of physical torture as punishment for chronically overdue patrons?

Eva, my head of circulation, claims that nickels and dimes are no longer effective in "getting the attention of the thirty to forty patrons who continually abuse our circulation rules and regulations." To my face, she has proposed a program of punishment whereby problem patrons will be forced to shelve books in order to retain their borrowing privileges, but behind my back I have heard that Eva and her circulation workers are fantasizing about certain forms of corporal punishment that were last used in Nazi Germany. I'll leave the details to your imagination.

But that's not the worst of it. Yesterday, when I walked into the staff lounge to get a cup of coffee I overheard Eva use the word "kill." Obviously, I am very concerned about my circulation staffers becoming obsessed or even adversarial with some of our more vexing patrons. I keep telling them not to worry about overdues, fines, and lost books, but they look at me with hatred in their eyes.

I have to do something before we have an unfortunate incident. I'm very concerned about obscene phone calls and nasty letters being exchanged. And who knows what could escalate from there?

Do you have any good advice on the care and feeding of circulation staffers?

Sincerely,
ON EDGE

Dear Edge,

First you have to realize that you are not alone. Circulation stress is an occupational hazard. It happens all the time. Perfectly normal people go to work in the circulation department of a library thinking that they are going to have a wonderful opportunity to work with people and books, and six months later they are prime candidates for psychological counseling.

The problem is that circulation staffers have to endure lie after lie about books that are lost ("I put the book in the bookdrop"), damaged ("somebody's dog must have gotten into your bookdrop"), and overdue ("I was in the hospital for three months for cancer surgery"). A few months of this duplicity and pretty soon that perfectly normal circ clerk begins to suspect that every library patron is either a thief, a prevaricator, or a procrastinator.

As a consequence, circ workers tend to have a very dim view about the future of Western Civilization. Their disillusionment develops into depression which evolves into hatred which we can hopefully stop from turning into violence. I have a bumber sticker that says "Keep Nuclear Weapons Away from Circulation Clerks."

In this context, the care and feeding of circ staffers (as you so aptly put it) is very important. Here are my tips: (a) assign the best parking spaces to circ workers, (b) provide them with free coffee, sugar, and cream for their workbreaks, (c) show them John Candy movies during their weekly staff meetings, (d) take them out to lunch on Valentine's Day, (e) take them to Happy Hour on St. Patrick's Day, (f) persuade your mayor to proclaim a "Circulation Staffers Appreciation Day," (g) give them chocolate once a week, (h) provide them with six free counseling sessions every year with a certified psychologist, and (i) let them take their birthdays off.

I hope this works for you.

Sincerely,
Will

Not Everyone Can Handle the Intensity of a Directorship

Dear Will,

I work in the reference department of a medium sized public library. The staff here is not what I would call one big happy family but for the most part we do have a warm and friendly working environment. My favorite part of the day is when five or six of us get together in the staff lounge for our mid-afternoon coffee break. It's a wonderfully relaxed time to review the events and the gossip of the day.

One of our favorite topics of conversation is our library director, Jonathan. He's a friendly, good-looking, and reasonably intelligent guy, but we know very little about him. The only time we get a chance to communicate with him is at our monthly staff meeting. Other than that he's fairly invisible.

So, Will, we were wondering what do library directors do all day?

Sincerely,

SYBIL

Dear Sybil,

Basically your average library director (1) gets to the office fashionably late, (2) pours himself a cup of coffee, (3) opens the newspaper ostensibly to scout out local news that might have an impact on the library but really to read the horoscope for the day, (4) pours another cup of coffee, (5) opens the mail, (6) calls Arnold over at Middleton Public to confirm their noon lunch date at the Rusty Scupper, (7) walks out to the car, (8) drives to the weekly meeting of the regional library directors council, (9) engages several other library directors in an intense discussion on the failings of the state library, (10) walks out to the car, (11) stops at the gas station for gas, (12) meets Arnold at the Rusty Scupper, (13) orders broiled sword-fish, (14) engages Arnold in an intense discussion on the failings of the regional library directors council, (15) shows great restraint by declining to take anything off the dessert cart, (16) gives in to a piece of carrot cake when Arnold decides to have a fudge brownie, (17) walks out to the car, (18) drives back to the office, (19) pours a cup of coffee, (20) opens the afternoon paper ostensibly to scout out late breaking local news that might have an impact on the library but really to check the evening's television listings, (21) walks out to the car, (22) drives to the State Library Association Headquarters to attend a meeting of the Municipal Library Administrators Round Table, (23) engages several of the administrators in an intense discussion of the failings of the county library, (24) walks out to the car, (25) drives back to the office, (26) calls Linda of Oakdale Public and confirms their agreement to meet for happy hour at Amnesia, (27) opens the evening newspaper ostensibly to check for late breaking

news that might have an impact on the library but really to read
"Far Side" and "Doonesbury," (28) walks out to the car, (29) drives to
Amnesia for happy hour, and (30) engages Linda in an intense
discussion on the failings of the Municipal Library Administrators
Round Table.

Regards,
Will

Index